BREAKING
THE
SURFACE

To Kara —
So glad to meet
you in person!
When it comes to
our relationship with
God, let's Go Deep!
Blessings,
Vicki J. Kuyper

Another New Hope book by Vicki J. Kuyper

Wonderlust: A Spiritual Travelogue for the Adventurous Soul

You can contact this author at www.vickikuyper.com.

BREAKING THE SURFACE

INVITING GOD *into the* SHALLOWS
AND THE DEPTHS *of* YOUR MIND

Vicki J. Kuyper

NEW HOPE
PUBLISHERS
Birmingham, Alabama

New Hope® Publishers
P. O. Box 12065
Birmingham, AL 35202-2065
www.newhopepublishers.com
New Hope Publishers is a division of WMU®.

Library of Congress Cataloging-in-Publication Data

Kuyper, Vicki J.
  Breaking the surface : inviting God into the shallows and the depths of your mind
/ Vicki J. Kuyper.
     p. cm.
  Includes bibliographical references (p.   ) and index.
  ISBN 978-1-59669-234-3 (sc : alk. paper)
  1. Spiritual life--Christianity. 2. Brain--Religious aspects--Christianity. I. Title.
  BV4509.5.K89 2008
  248.4--dc22

                              2008016265

ISBN-10: 1-59669-234-0
ISBN-13: 978-1-59669-234-3
N094131 • 1108 • 5M1

DEDICATION

To my amazing kids,
Katrina, Leticia, and my two Ryans.
May you never tire of setting your minds
on higher ground.

CONTENTS

ACKNOWLEDGMENTS

*"Every time your name comes up in my prayers,
I say, 'Oh, thank you, God!'"*
—Philemon 4 (*The Message*)

TO MY FIRST READERS:
Bridget, my "brain lady," thank you for helping me differentiate between my cerebral cortex and my frontal lobe.
Pam, thank you for being a faithful friend, as well as a faithful reader.
Karen, thank you for your honesty, integrity, passion, and gift of good words.
Rita, the "comma commando," thanks for caring about grammar, especially when I don't. (Or would that be "didn't"?)
Cynthia, your time may be limited, but the impact of your words on me is not. Thanks so much.

TO MY FAMILY:
Touchstones, one and all...mere words could never express the depth of my love and thanks.

TO THE STAFF AT NEW HOPE, MY CHURCH FAMILY, AND MY DEAR CIRCLE OF FRIENDS:
Your encouragement, companionship, and partnership undergird every word of this book.

Part 1

FISHING
FOR THE GREAT
I AM

CHAPTER ONE

GOD IS A SLIPPERY FISH

Set your mind on things above, not on earthly things.
—Colossians 3:2

God is a strong tower, a mighty warrior, a refuge, a shield, a solid rock. He's Someone who holds me close within the confines of sheltering wings.

Yes, God is all of these things. But He's also a slippery fish, swiftly squirming out of my toddlerlike fingers every time I catch a glimpse of His glory. He's a fish void of features or form, weight or color, size or sound. A fish with no beginning and no end. He's something I can't touch, taste, smell, hear, or see. How can I possibly keep my mind on something I can't hold in my hands or clearly picture in my thoughts? Every time I set my mind on God, He escapes my mental grasp and slips back beneath the surface of the racing stream that is my everyday life.

As for *"earthly things,"* as the Apostle Paul calls them, the nuts and bolts of my day-to-day existence, I don't need to fish for them. They jump into my thoughts without bidding.

It doesn't matter if I'm eating, praying, enjoying a movie, or trying to sleep—any time seems to be the right time for the bills that need to be paid, the growing mountain of laundry, or the cutting words someone tossed my way to leap back into my mind. They flop back and forth like glistening fish on a well-worn dock, gasping for breath, demanding my immediate attention. And if at that same moment I happen to have a tentative grasp on God, I often let Him go. God may be a slippery fish, but I'm also a distracted, inattentive fisherman.

I don't want God to be the One that got away. I don't want to tell fish stories to others, boasting about a God whom I've experienced more vicariously than personally. I want to set my mind and heart on Him as solidly as anyone still breathing a mortal breath can do. And I know I'm not alone.

You've felt it too. That tug at the line of your heart that lets you know there's something absolutely huge beneath the surface. Something of unimaginable power, beauty, and grace. Something you long to get close to, to catch a glimpse of, to take home with you, to show everyone you meet. But you're not sure you have the stamina and ability to reel it in.

The truth is, you don't. And neither do I. God is a slippery fish. And then again, He's not. He's also *not* a strong tower, a mighty warrior, or a solid rock. He's not even a "He" in the literal sense. These are only metaphors. God is something more. Something incomprehensibly unique. Something wholly divine. What God is, is the great I Am. He's beyond description. He's even beyond naming. Isaiah 46:5 (*The Message*) says, *"So to whom will you compare me, the Incomparable? Can you picture me without reducing me?"*

The only way our finite minds can catch a glimpse of our infinite God is to put Him in a box constructed of metaphor, a box the Almighty can't help but continually burst open at the hinges. That doesn't mean our word pictures are useless or erroneous. Even Jesus resorted to parables to help paint a picture for us of the invisible Father and His eternal kingdom.

But the words we have at our disposal are simply too small to contain God, as are our minds.

BIG GOD, SMALL BRAIN

Several years ago I had a dream. God and I were having a friendly chat. (I so wish I could remember what about!) I was seated at God's feet and He was dressed in the stereotypical white robe. But what I found most interesting, at least when I awoke, was that in my dream, God's head was missing. It seemed the "widescreen" of my dream simply wasn't big enough to contain Him, so it cut God off at the shoulders. Even in my wildest dreams, there's too much of God for me to grasp at one time.

I'm in good company. In Exodus 24:9–11, Moses and a large gathering of leaders all have the privilege of sharing a snack in God's presence. Even though the Bible states these men "*saw the God of Israel*," the only description we're given is of the sapphire pavement beneath God's feet—and chances are pretty good even these "feet" are metaphorical.

Later in Exodus 33, when Moses asks for a private showing of God's glory, God answers, as usual, in an unexpected way. First God displays His goodness. Then He announces His own name. Try putting yourself in Moses' sandals for just a moment. Experiencing the immensity of God's goodness buckles your knees with the weight of pure blessing. Then the verbal thunder of God declaring who He is quickens your heart with awe so unequaled you're not sure you'll survive another breath. The mind simply boggles. Talk about holy ground.

As if that's not enough, God then shields His chosen leader with His metaphorical hand, allowing Moses to catch only a quick glimpse of God's metaphorical back after the great I AM has passed by. Just that hint of glory is enough to set Moses's face aglow.

We have an incredibly big God—and a comparably itty-bitty brain. But God fashioned our brains according to the miraculous schematics of His own wise design. Somehow the big God, small brain combination is the perfect petri dish in which faith can grow.

But what about that inattentiveness I mentioned earlier? You'd think with a God this big—even if I couldn't fully understand Him—that the other stuff, those earthly things around me, wouldn't be a major distraction. After all, they can't hold a proverbial candle to the Light of the world. But earthly things have a one-up on God in one very important area. They are tangible. I can connect with them on a physical, experiential level. I can discern what they are like with my five senses. I can picture them in my memory long after my personal interaction with them has passed.

Try doing that with *"things above"*—heavenly things such as salvation, eternity, angelic beings, or God Himself. Setting my mind on them is like trying to contemplate the immensity of outer space. I get the basic concept, but if I try to wrap my mind around it—even using metaphor—I get tired after awhile. My mind begins to wander back to the things I can more easily relate to, back to my comprehensible, tangible "small brain" world.

THE TEFLON DILEMMA

OK, so my brain is small. But that's not all. It's also aging. Every day, every minute...there it goes again. Older yet. In my younger years, there were times when my mind bore a marked resemblance to Velcro. Everything it came into contact with stuck fast—telephone numbers, algebraic formulas, superfluous minutia. These days, my brain seems to have more in common with Teflon. Whatever I set on it slides right off. Even the names of friends I've known for years slip by like a fried egg off a nonstick pan in a late-night infomercial as I watch helplessly from the sidelines. I've come to accept that at this stage in my life, doing anything in addition to breathing seems to qualify as multitasking.

Yet forgetfulness is not just the bane of perimenopausal women. And it's not just a problem reserved for those who find themselves in the fast lane of a culture that seems to thrive on memory-taxing multitasking gone wild. History bears witness to the fact that the human race tends to be a forgetful lot. Even thousands of years ago, those living the Bible stories firsthand often had brains like a sieve. God brings ten plagues against the Egyptian Pharaoh, frees His people from the bondage of slavery, empowers Moses to divide the Red Sea, and provides manna and quail with the ease of fast food to the hungry Israelites wandering in a barren desert. But leave the same people who witness all of these miracles by themselves for a few days and the God they called *"my strength and my song"* slips their mind. In His place, they bow down to a lifeless, powerless image of a calf cast in gold.

The folks who lived in New Testament times were not much different. In the sixth chapter of Mark, the apostles witness how Jesus turns five loaves of bread and two fish into a picnic for more than 5,000 men (not including women and children), complete with 12 baskets of leftovers. A mere "two chapters" later, the apostles once again find themselves in the midst of a large, hungry crowd—and they begin to panic over the same "Lord, how shall we feed them?" problem. Could they really have forgotten the answer to that question so quickly?

But enough of picking on the people who had their spiritual foibles, along with their victories, recorded for posterity in Scripture. Are we really any different today? As we cruise out of the church parking lot, do we mutter under our breath about the driving habits of those who God commanded us to love "as we love ourselves"? After we close our Bibles and say our amens do the words God has spoken to us make any concrete difference in our day? When we come face-to-face with our own Red Sea, do we remember God's deliverance back in our own personal Egypt or start racing around searching for a pair of water wings?

I will be the first to admit, I've momentarily sold my soul for a hot fudge sundae. I've bowed down at the altar of "making a good impression." I've sought comfort from a sweater on a sales rack, instead of in the Everlasting Arms. Yes, I do know better. But sometimes I forget what I know. I forget the times God has come through in the past, as well as the power of His promises for my future. If I kept my mind on who God is and what I know of His goodness and grace, how could I possibly put anything or anyone in His place? Yet when earthly things tug at my heart, I often forget to hold on to what I know of God. He slips right out of my conscious thought and—at least for awhile—I carry on as though the things above have no bearing on my life below.

OK, so I'm scatterbrained as well as small-brained. I allow the little things right in front of me to block out the gigantic God all around me. Can you relate? Yet, despite all of our small-brained, distracted, forgetfulness, God is gracious. He knows us as profoundly as He loves us. That's why throughout history, God provided His people with touchstones, reminders that there is more to life than we can see with our eyes. But it's up to us whether we'll make use of them or not.

Touchstones from Heaven

In the Middle Ages, chemists and alchemists used touchstones to test the purity of gold and silver. When they dragged the black, flintlike stone across the surface of a potentially precious piece of metal, the mark that remained helped them differentiate between what was genuine and what was not. God's touchstones serve the same purpose. They point to what is real—even if it's beyond the scope of our senses.

Take God's covenant with Noah. God promises to never again flood the earth and destroy all life. Significant promise! Something you'd definitely want to remember, especially when dark storm clouds begin to build on the horizon. But God graciously gives Noah even more than His rock-solid word. God provides a touchstone crafted from the spectrum of light. Chances are from that day on every rainbow jogs Noah's memory. It was, and is, a visual symbol of something precious and real, God's promise and power. It reminds Noah that God cares.

Today, I'm in Nashville, Tennessee, far from my sunny, clear-skied home in Phoenix, Arizona. Throughout the state the storm clouds are building. A tornado watch and thunderstorm warning are in effect until late in the day. Schools are closing early and people are a bit on edge, waiting, watching. As I look out the window of my hotel room on the 19th floor, I scan the skies. I find myself searching for a rainbow as diligently as I'm watching for a funnel cloud. So far, I've seen nothing but a misty gray ceiling of clouds. But even without catching a glimpse of Noah's touchstone, just the memory of it keeps God in the forefront on my mind. No storm is more powerful than the God whom I serve, a God who cares for me and for each person in this storm's path.

Noah's touchstone was not just for Noah. It's for every generation after him who takes God's interaction with Noah to heart. Like Noah, we choose what we'll do when we catch sight of a rainbow in the sky. Will we use it as a touchstone? Will we allow it to help refocus our attention on God and His promises, on the things above we so easily forget? Will we simply ooh and aah over how lovely it is? Or will it barely stir a passing thought—because it is, after all, simply the scientific interaction between sunlight and showers?

It's true that a rainbow is just a band of colored light. Nothing more. But God embedded in it a deeper meaning and broader purpose that day with Noah. He did the same for the Israelites. By night, a pillar of fire was their rear guard. By day, a cloud moved before them, guiding their way. These two visible touchstones reminded God's people of His presence, protection, and promises in a supernatural way. But these touchstones were for a specific time, people, and purpose. They disappeared after the Israelites finally reached the Jordan River—and the Promised Land.

Sometimes God supplies the touchstone. Sometimes He asks His people to participate in its creation. And sometimes, people up and create a touchstone to help set their minds on things above just because they see the need. Take Samuel. When the Israelites soundly trounce the Philistines near Mizpah, Samuel set up a stone as a reminder of God's provision. Samuel even gives this literal touchstone a name: Ebenezer, meaning "stone of help." In 1 Samuel 7:12, Samuel declares, *"Thus far has the Lord helped us."*

But those were Old Testament times, right? With the exception of a few select leaders and prophets, God's Spirit dwelt *with* His people but not actually *in* them. Naturally the Israelites needed some additional help connecting with, and remembering, the invisible Creator of the universe. What about you and me? Jesus said the Counselor, God's Holy Spirit, would *"teach you all things and remind you of everything I have said to you"* (John 14:26). Jesus went on to say:

> *"When the Friend comes, the Spirit of Truth, he will take you by the hand and guide you into all the truth there is. He won't draw attention to himself, but will make sense out of what is about to happen and, indeed, out of all that I have done and said. He will honor me."*
> —John 16:13–14 (*The Message*)

God's Spirit is our own personal cloud by day and pillar of fire by night, our internal rainbow, our Ebenezer. He's our guide, our scriptural teleprompter, and our rock of remembrance. He's our touchstone pointing the way toward what is real and true, helping us separate eternal riches from the glitter of fool's gold. Unlike what happened to people in Old Testament times, God's Spirit never leaves us. We are His temple; His dwelling place; His living, breathing ark of the New Covenant. And still we forget...

But I know something rather significant about you, even though we've never met. If you're taking the time to read these words, I know you don't want your life, and your faith, to be characterized by forgetfulness. You want to hold on to God with all of your mental might, even though His unfathomable immensity makes Him seem rather slippery at times. You want to remember who He is, what He's done, and how close He is to you, more consistently throughout your day. You want to ponder things above, to overhaul negative thoughts with the power of what is true, noble, right, pure, lovely, admirable, excellent, and praiseworthy. And I want to help.

I want to invite you to journey beyond what is visible toward what is everlasting. We'll begin with a brief tour of our brains, the primary tool God has given us to use in seeking Him. Next, we'll explore in more depth how spiritual touchstones can help our small brains gain a firmer grasp on our big God. Then, we'll set sail for higher seas. We'll spend some time fishing for fresh insight into things above, using Philippians 4:8 to chart our course. Along the way, we'll gather personal touchstones to help us anchor what we learn more firmly into our thoughts and our lives.

So, why linger any longer? Let's go fish.

CHAPTER TWO

THIS IS YOUR BRAIN
ON GOD

*"Do not conform any longer to the pattern of this world,
but be transformed by the renewing of your mind."*
—Romans 12:2

God's divine design for the human brain is truly awe-
inspiring. It's the most complex organ in our bodies,
regulating virtually all of our activity. Every beat of our hearts,
every breath we take, every joke we tell, and every step of faith
we venture out on is dependent on this wrinkled, gelatinous,
network of neurons. And just like the rest of our body, our
brain benefits from exercise. So, put on your cerebral gym
shorts and prepare for a bit of a mental workout, because
we're going to take a whirlwind tour of God's brainchild—the
brain.

The brain is an information powerhouse. It transmits
data at over 200 miles per hour to our body's 100 billion
neurons, which are the cells of our nervous system. (And
in case 100 billion is a larger number than you can wrap
your mental mass around, that's somewhere in the vicinity of
the number of seconds that have passed since the end of the

last ice age...) This ongoing process generates enough raw energy that we could each power up our own individual 25-watt lightbulb.

Besides generating energy, our brain also generates thoughts and ideas. The individual human brain is capable of coming up with more thoughts than there are atoms in the known universe. To accomplish this monumental task, the mental power plant of our adult brain consumes 25 percent of our energy every day. (When we were infants and our brains were growing at an unprecedented pace, that percentage was closer to 60 percent!) Obviously, the brain has no trouble generating energy and ideas. But when it comes to *re*generating itself after an injury, things get a bit trickier. Unlike our skin and bones, the brain can't just grow more cells to heal. What the brain can do, depending on the damage it has suffered, is make new connections. Because of the brain's plasticity—it's ability to rewire and relearn—a stroke victim who is told he or she may never walk again may just prove the doctors wrong. Through conscious repetition of key actions and patterns, new pathways can open up in the brain. New connections can be made.

Likewise, every time we learn something new, come up with a fresh idea, or imprint another memory, we forge new neural connections in our brains. The more connections we make, the more efficient our brains become. God did not give people such as Albert Einstein, Leonardo da Vinci, and Stephen Hawking bigger brains than the rest of us. What sets geniuses like these apart from the average Joe or Josephine is the increased number of connections linked together in their brains. Want to follow in the footsteps of Einstein's neural paths? Build more connections.

So what does this little scientific lecture have to do with setting our minds on things above? A lot. The more connections we make in our brains between God and every other area of our lives, the harder it will be for Him to slip through our mental fingertips.

Sounds easy enough. But our brains face the same struggle as the rest of our bodies. When given the choice between being proactive or passive, we often choose comfort over effort. Before we know it, we become mental couch potatoes. Our minds slide into a rut etched out of habit and familiarity. We read Scripture we've read before without really thinking. We recite the requests on our prayer list like a kid who's asking a department store Santa for toys—but who no longer believes the "big guy" is for real. We sit in the same seat in church every Sunday, expecting the worship songs and pastor's sermon to fire up our spiritual batteries, without plugging in our own heart, soul, mind, and strength. And we wonder why God feels so far away.

In 1 Corinthians 14:15 Paul writes, *"I will pray with my spirit, but I will also pray with my mind; I will sing with my spirit, but I will also sing with my mind."* Though this verse is part of a discussion on the gift of tongues and its place in church, I believe Paul's words apply to every area of our spiritual lives. We cannot wholly follow God if our minds aren't paying attention to where we're headed. Like a car whose inattentive driver isn't watching the road, we could end up drifting outside our given lane.

When we follow the same routine day after day, both spiritually and physically, it's like a long, boring car trip—and our brains adjust to the lazy, inattentive pace. The less stimulation, the fewer new connections. Our brain waves may not be flatlining, but our learning curve certainly is.

God's character may be as unchanging as a rock, but that doesn't make Him boring. Relationships are dynamic, active, challenging, and surprising. Our relationship with the God of the universe should certainly be nothing less! So how do we fight atrophy and promote growth in our relationship with God? One way is to climb out of our religious rut. Shake things up a bit. Make some new mental connections.

Association is the blowtorch for forging new mental connections. We make associations by connecting something new to something old, linking unfamiliar information or experience to something we already know or have done. We categorize it, organize it, and figure out where we're going to store it. We study it from every angle via our senses. How does this thing look, taste, smell, sound, feel? What is it like? How is it unique? If we are surprised by what we learn, or if there are very strong emotions intertwined with the information we're taking in, our new memory imprints itself a bit more securely in our mental files. And the more mental file folders we associate with this new memory, the easier it will be for us to retrieve it, whether voluntarily or involuntarily. Most of this happens without us ever really paying much attention to what's going on. But what if we did? What if we intentionally chose to forge more mental connections with things above? I believe we'd begin to experience the true power behind Romans 12:2. We'd conform to a new perspective and pattern of thinking. We'd be transformed by the renewing of our minds.

RENEWAL THROUGH REWIRING

Our brains are far from fixed or static. Researcher and psychiatrist Norman Doidge, MD, author of *The Brain That Changes Itself*, states that "the brain is constantly rewiring itself." He claims that patterns ingrained in our minds can be changed and new ones forged, but that rewiring these neural connections requires self-motivation. However, I believe self-motivation is just the beginning. When we add God's participation to our own personal motivation, then this "rewiring" has the potential to rise to the heights of renewal, transforming both our lives and our relationship with God.

Setting our minds on things above is both a gift and a choice. As the Holy Spirit brings to mind God's words and His ways, we can let them flow over our God-parched lives like a refreshing mountain stream. Then we can quickly shake ourselves off, letting the truth roll right off of our minds as we continue on our way—refreshed but unchanged. Or, we can choose to bask a bit longer, to make deeper, more enduring mental connections. We can choose to be renewed instead of merely refreshed. We can ask ourselves, "How does this relate to what I know? To what I've experienced? Is there anything I can see, feel, touch, taste, hear, or smell that I can associate with this truth? How can I make a lasting memory?"

From a scientific point of view, the memories we make are classified as either episodic or semantic. Episodic memories are those in which you have a starring role. They are the scrapbook of your experiences. They not only contain what happened at a given time, but the context that surrounded the event—how what happened affected you. These memories may, or may not, be totally in line with reality. They are your perceived reality of your personal experiences, your inner autobiography.

On the other hand (or part of the brain, as the case may be), semantic memory stores general, instead of personal, knowledge. Facts and figures, words and their meanings, anything that doesn't need to be tied to an event to be understood are all classified as semantic memories.

The reasons we forget episodic and semantic memories are vast and varied. But since this is not a college class on the physiology of the brain, we're going to focus on two common causes. First, when a memory isn't exercised—taken out for a mental stroll once in awhile—it's more easily forgotten. Secondly, as we acquire new memories, they tend to make room on our mental hard drives by erasing what's old and outdated. The less relevant something is to us personally (that means the fewer associations it has to our episodic memory), the more quickly it seems to be weeded out. In other words, both repetition and relevance (in addition to forging a strong network of mental connections through association) seem to be vital keys to building lasting memories—any kind of memories, including those that draw our minds to things above over and over again.

Using repetition as a memory aid is certainly not a novel concept. If you want to memorize a new phone number, or the Gettysburg Address, replaying what you're trying to learn over and over in your head is fairly intuitive. Of course, once you stop revisiting what you've memorized, it can slide off your mental radar screen rather quickly—and chances are the reason you stopped revisiting what you learned was because it was no longer relevant. The friend whose phone number you memorized moved away—or is now on speed dial. The play you learned all those lines for had its final curtain call. The verse of Scripture you memorized with your Bible study group slipped from sight, and thought, once you began studying a new topic.

My son, Ryan, once learned close to 100 Scripture verses over a few short weeks. He visited a Bible club at a friend's church that offered kids a piece of candy for every verse they memorized. That was all it took for Ryan to became a Scripture memory machine. He started the "summer challenge" three weeks late, but soon caught up with, and passed, most of the rest of the kids in the club. Ryan could rattle off any verse the leader mentioned on cue. Unfortunately, once the competition (and the free candy) ended, so did Ryan's incentive. The verses slipped out of Ryan's head as quickly as they had entered it. Ryan mastered repetition, but had totally sidestepped relevance.

God is not a project. He is a Person (metaphorically speaking, yet again.) All of this talk of repetition, rewiring, neural pathways, building associations, and our part in securing long-lasting memories can twist our focus toward nurturing knowledge over relationship. Yes, there are steps we can take to help us draw closer to God with our minds. But instead of a how-to course, my hope is this one-sided discussion will be more of a "who will you turn to?" catalyst. Knowing more *about* God is important. But knowing *Him* will always reign supreme.

Relevance is what keeps God from being exiled to our semantic memory. He is not a list of commandments or a file folder of facts. He is love. If we want Him to become a broader, more vital part of our episodic memory, we need to allow Him to step out from the pages of Scripture and into our everyday lives. We need to examine how and why He is relevant to us individually. Then we need to reflect on what we learn. Mull it over. Ponder. Ruminate. Meditate. Remember.

To researchers who study the brain, personalizing associations is called *deep processing*. To me, when this process relates to God, it's simply spending time with the One I love. I never meditate on things above alone. My rumination is a running conversation with God. And I find that touchstones, along with being memory joggers, make great conversation starters.

Deep "C" Fishing

At the end of each chapter, "Deep 'C' Fishing" will offer you the chance to dive a bit deeper into your cerebrum. (OK, I know you're rolling your eyes at me. So what if puns and wordplay are often referred to as the lowest form of humor? They can also be a mnemonic device. So, please cut me some literary slack—and just be thankful I didn't go with "Hook, Line, and Thinker.")

If you want to remember what you read, you need to act on what you've just heard. Talk about it. Write about it. Adopt a new touchstone into your life. Take a more in-depth look at how what you've read can be applied to your life.

Here's your chance:

1. James 1:22–24 (*The Message*) says: "*Don't fool yourself into thinking that you are a listener when you are anything but, letting the Word go in one ear and out the other. Act on what you hear! Those who hear and don't act are like those who glance in the mirror, walk away, and two minutes later have no idea who they are, what they look like.*"

- How does what you've just learned about the brain support what this Scripture says?

- What would you most like to remember from what you've just read? What action are you going to take to help you do just that?

2. Research shows that students do not retain the most information about a teacher's lecture immediately after hearing it, but 10 minutes later! That's because the brain takes about 10 minutes to associate everything it's just heard in a 40- to 60-minute lecture with what it already knows—to build new connections and relate the material to the student's own personal experience. However, after 10 minutes, a student's memory starts to fade.

- How can you use this information to change what you do after listening to a sermon at church? After studying Scripture? After reading a chapter in this book?

3. Elaboration is a mnemonic device that can help you build associations between new information and what you already know. One method of elaboration is to paint a picture in your mind of what you want to remember. The picture doesn't have to make logical sense. Remember, the element of surprise can actually aid in memory retention! Try and paint a mental picture of Isaiah 26:3 (TNIV): *"You will keep in perfect peace those whose minds are steadfast, because they trust in you."*

- My mental picture was of myself resting on a hammock with a vise on my head (that's my image of a steadfast mind!) and God's huge, metaphorical hands holding up either side of the hammock, swaying it slowly. How about yours?

- Since you know how important repetition and relevance are to securing things above in your memory, take a few moments to mull this image, and its meaning, over in your mind. How is this verse of Scripture relevant to you? What difference does this truth make in your life?

- For the next week, every evening right before you go to sleep, call this image to mind and ponder the promise of Isaiah 26:3. At the end of the week write in a journal, or share with a friend, what God has taught you through these two verses.

CHAPTER THREE

REMEMBER ME

"Do this in remembrance of me."
—Luke 22:19

The wine, the bitter herbs, the unleavened bread...the disciples know the routine. They've eaten this meal before. They've contemplated the Israelites' bitter bondage in Egypt and their hasty escape to the wilderness. They've celebrated God's deliverance from death through the unlikely "savior" of a lamb's blood on a doorframe. They've recalled the story of the birth of the Hebrew nation. How could they forget it? They've heard it over and over again since childhood. But tonight that story's being rewritten. And the lives of John, Peter, Judas, and the rest of the Twelve are each being written right into it.

There are murmurs. Quizzical looks. Forthright questions. Confusion. One disciple abruptly leaves the table, raising yet more conjecture and queries. Jesus quietly picks up the unleavened bread. With a word of thanks to His heavenly Father, He rips it apart. Then He pauses, looking down at the bread He holds in His hands. Stray crumbs fall to the floor. Ragged edges mark the place where one whole has been torn in two. Jesus raises His eyes to meet those of his friends reclined around the table. "Do this in remembrance of me."

Huh?

If that expression has an Aramaic counterpart, I'm fairly certain it was one of the first words that crossed the disciples' bewildered minds. The disciples were prepared for ritual. What Jesus offered was renewal. A new twist on an old tale. A new covenant in place of the old. A new touchstone for a new generation. Chances are good that every person in that room never looked at a Passover meal the same way again—or even bread and wine, for that matter. And we're offered that same opportunity.

Of course, what was a new story to Jesus's disciples can all too easily become an old story to us. If we let it.

But at the Last Supper, Jesus gave us more than a story. He gave us a touchstone. Instead of passively listening to Jesus interact with His chosen Twelve by reading Scripture, we're invited to join their ranks and partake of the meal firsthand. We have the chance to see, touch, smell, and even taste God's new covenant with us. Is it any coincidence that is precisely how lasting memories are made?

TOUCHSTONES 101

All of this talk of touchstones may be new to you. Or you may be like me—your house may be filled with memorabilia. My collection includes treasures such as my love-worn teddy bear from childhood, a Fox Mulder action figure from my *X-Files* addiction days, and a set of piranha teeth I brought back from my life-changing adventure to a survival camp in the Amazon.

Regardless if your treasures bear any resemblance to mine or not, if you have photo albums you leaf through to relive memories of good times with those you love, if you have a box of baby clothes you've saved to remind yourself how quickly time flies, if you have a trophy on display that heralds a past victory in the business world or on a sports field, or if you wear a wedding ring, you understand the concept. These items are more than knickknacks or souvenirs. They are memory joggers extraordinaire. They are keepsakes tied to something significant in our lives. They point our minds backwards toward something we don't want to lose touch with. They help us remember what we believe matters most.

I received my first spiritual touchstone the day I received Christ into my heart. It was at a Christian camp on an inlet of the Saltery Bay in British Columbia. Although it was summer, the afternoon was gloomy. A damp gray veil of mist hung low to the water. It was the final day of camp and our afternoon activity was to find a quiet spot to talk to God about what we'd learned over the last seven days.

Still searching for that "perfect shell" I'd been looking for all week, I decided to head down to a rocky slice of beach in a sheltered cove. I scoured the slate-colored sand for a shell that was more than a fragment. Nothing. I sat down on the soggy mix of sand and stones, cross-legged, head in my hands—and rather matter-of-factly introduced myself to the God of the universe.

We'd chatted briefly before. I'd attended the Catholic Church until I was 12 and I knew my Hail Marys and Our Fathers. I'd called out for "help" a time or two over the years when I didn't know where else to turn. And on occasion, I'd found myself thanking Someone for a stellar sunset or the tympanic lightning strikes of a thunderstorm that made me shudder with a combination of awe and delight. But I'd never really talked like this . . . Candidly. Conversationally. Vulnerably. Ready to commit my life to Someone I couldn't even see with my eyes or embrace with my arms.

The only reason I'd signed up for camp was I heard it had great waterskiing. The promotional film I'd seen in my high school psychology class (how times have changed!) did show some teenagers studying the Bible, but I figured that activity was probably optional. But once I arrived, someone handed me an actual Bible. Being the insatiable reader that I am, I started to do a little reading on my own. The Bible was different from any other book I'd ever read. Although centuries old, the words felt like they were written to me. Here was an Author I wanted to get to know personally.

I shared that desire in prayer on the beach. Almost immediately the sound of laughter, a coed mix of teenage giggles and shouts, arose from a bit farther down the shore. "Please, Lord," I asked. "Help them forget about playing for awhile and find You." It was my first intercessory prayer.

When I opened my eyes, there it was. The perfect shell nestled right between my feet. How I could I have missed it moments before? A word of thanks tumbled over my lips. Here I was, a newborn child of God, and already receiving gifts. My very first spiritual touchstone.

Over 30 years later, that snow-white shell still has the power to transport me to a foggy shoreline and urge my lips toward words of praise. It's a tangible reminder of how the God my heart had secretly been searching for since the day I was born had been right under my nose the whole time. In its own unique way, this simple shell continues to softly whisper, "Remember Me."

Spiritual touchstones may point our minds back, but ultimately they should point our minds up. They should remind us there is more to life than meets our eye. There is a Creator behind creation. Spiritual battles being fought. Eternal destinies at risk. Heavenly involvement in earthly affairs. Love itself, alive and omnipresent, reaching out to the world with an invisible Hand. A plan in place in which we play a vital part. Truth—not always evident in circumstance—that proclaims we are precious, God is good, and in the end all will be made right once more.

The more conscious we are of the bigger picture, of the overarching spiritual dimension that reaches beyond what we can see, hear, feel, touch, and taste, the more natural it feels to "walk by faith." As our minds are renewed by a higher perspective our hearts are transformed for an eternal purpose. And that's when we start to notice something has changed: "things above" seem to intersect and connect more frequently with our lives below.

Spiritual touchstones can play a part in this process by acting as a memory aid, kind of like a mnemonic device. They come in countless shapes, sizes, and forms, as varied as our individual creativity and experience. They can be as familiar as taking part in communion or baptism. They can be a visual "string around our finger," like Noah's rainbow, a reminder of what God has done. They can be something tangible we can hold in our hands, like the tassels on the Israelites' clothing. Here's how *The Message* describes those tassels:

> GOD spoke to Moses: "Speak to the People of Israel. Tell them that from now on they are to make tassels on the corners of their garments and to mark each corner tassel with a blue thread. When you look at these tassels you'll remember and keep all the commandments of GOD, and not get distracted by everything you feel or see that seduces you into infidelities. The tassels will signal remembrance and observance of all my commandments, to live a holy life to GOD."
> —Numbers 15:37–40

Touchstones can come to us courtesy of God, like His tassels directive. Or we can choose to implement our own personal touchstones, like me and my shell or Samuel and his Ebenezer. A touchstone can even be as intangible as a metaphor—"God is my rock." Whatever form a spiritual touchstone takes, its job is to serve as a jumper cable to jolt our brain back to thinking about God and *"things above."*

What a touchstone is *not* is a talisman, nor is it a lucky rabbit's foot. Touchstones have no intrinsic worth, other than to jog our memories. They are not sacred. They do not wield special power or entitle us to special favor. Although Samuel's

Ebenezer was significant to him, it was really just a rock. We may get all sentimental over some spiritual touchstones God uses mightily in our lives, but in the end they are just tools. Regarding them as anything more risks their elevation to the level of idols in our hearts.

In Judges 8:22–27, Gideon falls into this very trap. Gideon, a shrinking-violet farmer whom God transforms into His mighty warrior, does a lot of things right (as noted in Judges 6–8). Gideon tears down an altar for idol worship built by his own dad. Gideon builds an altar to God and names it *"The Lord is Peace"* (Judges 6:24). He reduces the number of his army to a mere pittance so that their defeat of the Midianites can only be attributed to the power of God and not their own strength. He turns down the Israelites' request for him to become king, insisting that only God should rule over them.

But in the very next breath, Gideon gets off track. He takes his mind off things above and slips back into the pattern of the world, those *"earthly things"* (remember Colossians 3:2?), back into a self-centered cycle of power, pride, and greed. All he does is ask the Israelites for one little favor. After all, he did humbly turn down their fabulous offer to become their illustrious ruler. The least they can do is each give him one gold earring from the plunder they've taken.

With his 43 pounds of gold earrings, Gideon decides to make an *ephod*—a priest's "apron." Back in the Book of Exodus, God introduced the ephod as a sacred touchstone for priests. It was part of a fancy waistcoat ensemble, imbedded with precious stones bearing the names of the twelve tribes. This ensemble also held some mysterious things called the Urim and Thummin. The high priests used these to discern God's will in certain situations.

Gideon's golden ephod may have started out as a touchstone. He may have intended it to be a kind of monument designed to point people's attention toward God. But Gideon twisted God's original intent. Gideon wasn't a priest and the ephod wasn't going to be used as a sacred vestment. As a result, Judges 8:27 says, *"All Israel prostituted themselves by worshiping it [the ephod] there, and it became a snare to Gideon and his family."* In the end, Gideon ended up following in the footsteps of his earthly father, instead of His heavenly one. He led his own people to worship an idol. Even good intentions can head the wrong direction once we lose our focus on things above.

Personally, I have found the use of touchstones to be a valuable memory aid to me through the years. They have helped remind me of God's victories in my life, promises He's made and kept, and truths about who God is and who He says I am. They've helped pull my anxious thoughts out of a downward worry spiral. They've prompted me to raise my voice in praise, bend my knees in prayer, reach out to someone in love, and wipe tears from my eyes as my heart overflowed with gratitude. Touchstones are ordinary things that help point me toward the extraordinary. But they've never changed my life. Only God can do that.

Second Corinthians 5:7 (NKJV) clearly states, *"We walk by faith, not by sight."* Even though "out of sight, out of mind" may more accurately describe our walk with our heavenly Father at times, touchstones are simply signposts along the road of life, pointing our minds upward. Our faith lies in God alone, not in what points us to Him.

I BREAK FOR TOUCHSTONES

Let's pause for a moment and practice a little of that repetition we talked about earlier. We've looked at two significant topics: the mechanics of how our brains work and how touchstones (used in a God-honoring way) can act as conduits between our lives "here below" and *"things above."* Before we continue down this informational highway, let's head back to the table of the Last Supper.

In light of everything you've read, take a fresh look at God's touchstone of communion. Jesus offers us a multisensory experience, just as He did His first-century followers. He invites us to *"take and eat."* To hold the bread and the cup in our hands. See the blood-colored hue of the wine or juice. Smell the bread as we lift it to our lips and taste it as it dissolves in our mouths. Hear Jesus's words as they were recorded in the Gospels, just as the disciples heard them firsthand. Associate Jesus and His New Covenant with what we already know of the Passover and God's promise for a Messiah—make what is old relevant to us today. Celebrate this "communion" not as a one-time event, but over and over again through our lives. This is what Jesus tells his first-century disciples, and us, to do to remember Him.

What an infinitely wise and wonderful God we serve! A big God who helps our small brains recall what He's done for us in ways that uniquely fit the way He designed our brains to learn. Ways that fight off forgetfulness. Ways that encourage us to follow His example! He helps us build new associations through our senses, make something familiar more spiritually relevant in our lives, and then encourages us to eat—and repeat.

If what you've read so far has made you think about the Lord's Supper, and touchstones, in a new way, some neural rewiring has already begun to take place. But why stop there? You can build an additional link of connection by acting on what you've just learned.

Movement is like a sixth sense when it comes to memory. Along with touch, taste, sight, smell, and hearing, movement is a file folder that helps strengthen the neural filing system of memories we are trying to retain. Why do you think teachers combine hand movements with Bible songs for kids in Sunday School? For the same reason I have to squelch the urge to stamp my feet anytime I hear "Father Abraham had many sons." Movement is a great memory aid. It's so good that simply mentioning that annoying ditty has resurrected Father Abraham from a seldom used file cabinet buried somewhere in the deepest recesses of my mind—and now I can't seem to get him to march back to where he belongs. If only I could choose what to forget! But that's another story.

Breaking the Surface

Today we are choosing to act on what we long to remember. And that's why I did what I just did. After writing about the touchstone of communion, I felt compelled to follow my own advice. I didn't plan it. It wasn't listed on my outline or scheduled into my day. I didn't do it because I thought it would make a more vivid illustration in this book. I did it because I saw an opportunity to connect with God, to momentarily set my mind on things above. So, I stopped writing and took action.

Since I have neither wine nor grape juice on hand, I filled a fancy glass (the ones that only come out when company sits around our table) with water. I took an "unleavened" cracker from the pantry. I grabbed my Bible and headed outside to the stone table on the patio.

It's hot today. Already over 100°F, even though summer won't officially start for almost a month. But I wanted to pull myself out of the comfort of my air-conditioned home office. I wanted to make a conscious choice to be more aware of my surroundings. I wanted to remember Jesus, His sacrifice, and His covenant in a new way. And I did.

I added another file folder to my growing mental library. I embedded God a little more securely into my brain, made a few more associations, wired a few fresh neural connections. But most importantly, I spent time with Someone I love.

My hope is that my words will inspire you to do the same—to draw even closer to your true soul Mate. To knit things above more seamlessly into your life below. To take a fresh look at familiar Christian rituals. To find your thoughts "straying" more consistently toward what's of eternal worth. To persevere in holding on to the slippery fish of faith. And to begin to gather some touchstones of your own into your mental memory basket.

How you'll go about gathering touchstones will be as unique as the touchstones themselves. Don't be afraid to let your imagination come out and play. (Remember, God has given you the capability to generate more thoughts than there are atoms in the universe!) The biblical examples and personal experiences throughout this book are designed to prime your brain, helping you better see potential touchstones all around you. But if you find yourself baffled by where to begin, ask God to provide something to help bring Him to mind more regularly. You may just find a white shell between your toes.

Of course, the first thing you notice when you decide to work hand in hand with God to set your mind on things above is that *"things above"* covers a lot of territory. As we said before, trying to set our minds on what is limitless and eternal is beyond the scope of the brain God has given us to work with.

To aid us in our ongoing big God, small brain dilemma, we'll use Philippians 4:8 as our fishing net. Naturally, our infinite God can't possibly be contained within it, but choosing to focus our minds on whatever is true, noble, right, pure, lovely, admirable, excellent, and praiseworthy is a good place to start. After all, Philippians 4:8 is one of the mental fishing holes God has explicitly directed us to in Scripture. Here we'll fish for insight, relevance, and renewal—along with a little neural rewiring. But most of all, we'll keep our eyes and hearts open for a glimpse of the One we don't want to get away... our strong tower, our mighty warrior, our refuge, our strength, our Creator and Lord—the one and only I Am.

Deep "C" Fishing

Chances are you've used a spiritual touchstone at some point in your relationship with God, but you may have never looked at it from the same angle that we did in this chapter. Let's delve a little deeper into the biblical precedent for touchstones—and in considering how ritual can lead us into a rut—or onto the road to renewal.

1. Though the word *touchstone* is never used in the Bible, examples of touchstones are scattered throughout its pages.

   • What are a few examples you can think of that were not mentioned in this chapter? If you get stuck, take a look at Genesis 28:10–22; Exodus 13:1–16; Exodus 16:33–34; Numbers 10:8–10; Deuteronomy 27:1–8; Malachi 3:14–16; Matthew 3:11; or Matthew 9:1–7.

   • Are there any touchstones you use regularly, or have used in the past, to help you focus on God?

2. For many people, the word *ritual* has a lot of baggage attached to it. But rituals and traditions can be useful touchstones, if we don't fall into the habit of just going through the motions. Consider what Jesus has to say to the Pharisees in Mark 7:6–7 (TNIV):

"Isaiah was right when he prophesied about you hypocrites; as it is written: 'These people honor me with their lips, but their hearts are far from me. They worship me in vain; their teachings are merely human rules.' You have let go of the commands of God and are holding human traditions."

- What spiritual rituals do you participate in or have taken part of in the past? What do you believe makes a spiritual ritual or tradition valuable?

- What can you do to make these rituals a more relevant, and memorable, part of your spiritual life?

- Do any of Jesus's words to the Pharisees strike a chord in your own life?

3. The word *remember* is used about 150 times in the Bible (and is mentioned over 100 times more if you include variations of the word in your calculations!). We're encouraged to remember lots of things, some more naturally memorable

than others. These include the Sabbath day (Exodus 20:8), the wonders God has done (1 Chronicles 16:12), Lot's wife (Luke 17:32), it's more blessed to give than receive (Acts 20:35), the poor (Galatians 2:10), your Christian leaders (Hebrews 13:7), past generations (Deuteronomy 32:7), and to thank God for those He's used as blessings in our lives (Philippians 1:3).

- Choose one eternally significant thing above you would like to secure more firmly in your memory—and in your life. Then, find a touchstone to help cement this concept a little better in your cerebrum. You could choose a physical touchstone (like my seashell), paint a mental picture through elaboration (like rocking in a hammock held by the hands of God), participate in a spiritual ritual (like communion), or even sing aloud a new song. (If you have trouble coming up with a tune, "Father Abraham" is always memorable!)

Part 2

GATHERING
TOUCHSTONES

CHAPTER FOUR

WHO AM I AND
WHO'S THE GREAT I AM?

"Whatever is true."
—Philippians 4:8

What is truth?

Talk about opening a can of worms. But if we're going fishing for the great I AM, it's good to bring along a worm or two. Or if you're like me, a tackle box full. Worms are the questions that make us squirm. They're the bait we put on the line, dangle before God, and then wait for Him to answer. They are the hows and whys and why nots of living in a "big God, small brain" world. God's truth may be absolute, but it certainly isn't crystal clear. But that doesn't mean it's so high above us we can't set our minds on it—even if our minds do tend to slide off of it now and again.

Truth calls things the way they really are, both seen and unseen. Truth deals in reality. And let's face it, if we're not going to deal with reality, why deal at all? Psalm 19:4 (*The Message*) reminds us that *"unspoken truth is spoken everywhere."* God has embedded truth into creation, as well as into His Word.

Though truth is evident here on earth, its evidence draws our minds to things above, which in turn draws us straight to God.

"*Whatever is true*" gives us enough to set our minds on from now until Jesus returns. But we're going to narrow that focus, at least somewhat. We're going to focus on the truth about who we are and who God is. OK, so that's *still* enough to chew on with our mental molars until we meet Jesus face-to-face. Now, if only we could stop ourselves from getting distracted.

THE ME I WAS CREATED TO BE

"Well, it's, uh, bigger than I pictured it would be." I could tell my husband was choosing his words as carefully as an explosives expert chooses which wire to cut when diffusing a bomb. After 20 years of marriage, my husband knew his response had the potential to be a peace offering or a weapon of mass destruction. He chose wisely—balancing truth with neutrality.

The guys at the tattoo parlor had been more outright complimentary. "Beautiful!" declared a leather-clad biker with a ZZ Top beard watching from an adjacent tattoo booth. I had to smile, despite the annoying prick of the needle injecting permanent ink beneath my skin. *Beautiful! That's what God says about me,* I thought. That was the reason I chose to get a tattoo in the first place.

The Bible proclaims that we are "*God's masterpiece*" (Ephesians 2:10 NLT). But for years that truth seemed to slip my mind every time I looked in the mirror. I could blame it on low self-esteem, comparing myself with models in magazines, or allowing years of critical words to take root in my heart. Whatever the reason, accepting the physical frame God chose to display the "masterpiece of me" in has always been an all-out struggle.

So one day I decided to have a heart-to-heart with the Artist. I asked God how *He* saw me. As I prayed, the image of a wildflower formed in my mind's eye. It was delicate in design, yet dazzling in its simple splendor, robed in royal purple petals—attire wholly appropriate for a child of the King. God reminded me that individual wildflowers don't stand out in a crowd. They blend in with the field around them. But if you take the time to get up close enough to study a single blossom, there will be no question as to its beauty.

From that day forward, purple flowers and I had a connection. Every one was a touchstone, a reminder of who I really was. When potted African violets went on sale at the grocery store, I bought them. (Unfortunately, they shriveled to skeletal brown twigs within a matter of weeks because houseplants and I really do not have a healthy working relationship.) When a single purple wildflower courageously burst through a crack in our driveway I carefully drove around it, celebrating its beauty until it was pummeled to smithereens by hail. When I saw real wildflowers, purple alyssum, preserved and made into a pair of earrings—and read that the flower stood for "worth beyond beauty"—I whipped out my credit card. And when my daughter and I decided to celebrate her 16th birthday by both getting tattoos (yes, there is so much more to this story), the image of a purple wildflower was the only design choice for me.

Now, whenever I catch sight of the wildflower on my shoulder, I'm reminded of who I really am. I'm a child of the King, with beauty interwoven both into what can be seen and what cannot, a work of art more precious to God than any literal lily of the field.

Do I always feel like God's masterpiece? Beautiful? Treasured? Of incalculable worth? Not always, but more often than not. And when I do forget who I am and begin to question my self-worth, the image of a purple wildflower appears in my mind. Somehow, in my mental file folders, my view of myself and God's view of me seem to be more permanently cross-referenced since I got my tattoo. I pull up one folder and the other comes up right along with it. I still have the choice to believe what I read in those files or not, but the truth is right there in front of me. That makes it harder to forget.

Not everyone needs, or wants, a tattoo touchstone. Some people even believe it goes against the Bible to have one. Some quote Leviticus 19:28, *"Do not cut your bodies for the dead or put tattoo marks on yourselves. I am the LORD."* Back in Old Testament times, tattooing or painting the body had religious significance in the neighboring pagan cultures, so the Israelites were told not to do it. Of course, I live in New Testament times and am no longer under the burden of the countless laws recorded in Leviticus. Jesus took care of that once and for all. But for those who question my choice in getting a tattoo, I point to the verse right before the mention of tattoos. Leviticus 19:27 says, *"Do not cut the hair at the sides of your head or clip off the edges of your beard."* Men usually change the subject at this point. As for women, I point them up a bit further to verse 19, which reads, *"Do not wear clothing woven of two kinds of material."* It's hard to imagine they've never donned a poly-cotton blend. But I digress...

For me, my tattoo touchstone is reminiscent of the way God changed people's names throughout Scripture. For the people of Israel, names were more than just something you called someone. A name expressed something significant about a person's history or character. For instance, *Moses* means "taken from the water." *Jacob* means "he grasps the heel," which is exactly what Jacob did to his twin brother Esau's foot at birth. "He grasps the heel" is also a figurative turn of phrase meaning "he deceives," which Jacob proceeded to do to his father and brother later in life.

In Genesis 17, God changes the name of *Abram*, which means "exalted father," to *Abraham*, which means "father of many." God changes Abraham's name after Ishmael is conceived, but before Sarai (whom God renames *Sarah*) actually becomes pregnant with Isaac. It's a name that foreshadows the great things to come. It's interesting to note that *Sarai* means "my princess," while *Sarah* means "a princess." By changing the last letter of Sarai's name, God transformed Abraham's "princess" to a princess who would become the mother of future kings and princes for everyone—not the least of which would be the Prince of Peace Himself.

The Prince of Peace followed in His heavenly Father's name-changing footsteps. During Jesus's very first encounter with Simon, Jesus changed His future disciple's name to Peter. *Peter* (*Cephas* in Aramaic) means "a rock or a fragment of a rock." No longer would Simon be referred to only as the son of John. Instead he would be known as a "piece of the rock." The rock Peter was part of was Christ Himself—the cornerstone (1 Peter 2:7 NKJV) for those who choose to believe in God, and a stumbling block (1 Peter 2:8) for those who do not.

What's in a Name?

If life were a comic book, Simon would be a superhero who discovers his true identity in John 1:42. For years Simon believed he was a simple fisherman, the son of John. So did everyone else. But then Simon meets a wise teacher named Jesus. Jesus reveals to Simon who he really is, the hero God created him to be. Instead of giving Simon a spandex suit and cape, Jesus provides him with something more powerful. He bestows on Simon his true name.

Every time the hero-formerly-known-as-Simon hears someone call him Peter, he's reminded of the important part he's destined to play, a part in a story much larger than his own individual chapter. Peter is reminded he's more than the son of John. He's a child of the all-powerful God—a genuine chip off the old Rock.

Remember, to the people of Israel, an individual's name was more than just an arbitrary moniker. A child's name was a statement about his or her character, lineage, or life circumstances. Just look at the name-calling that goes on between Leah and Rachel as they try to one-up each other through childbirth in Genesis 29 and 35. First Leah gives birth to a son, an apparent consolation prize for a loveless marriage. Leah names him *Reuben*, which means, "See, a son!" Barren Rachel responds by handing her maidservant over to her husband, Jacob, in hopes of a surrogate birth. This produces *Dan*, meaning "He [God] has vindicated me!"

When Leah can longer bear children, she follows Rachel's example and hands off her maidservant to Jacob. Son *Gad* is the result, meaning "what good fortune!" After the baby battle between Jacob's wives and his maidservants produces 11 sons and 1 daughter, 1 final son is born to favored wife, Rachel. As she's dying in childbirth, she names the child *Ben-Oni*, meaning "son of my trouble." But after Rachel dies, Jacob quickly changes his son's name to *Benjamin*, meaning "son of my right hand."

What would it be like to grow up as "son of my trouble"? Or *Delilah*, possibly meaning "temptress"? Or *Esau*, meaning "hairy"? Or *Ish-Bosheth*, meaning "man of shame"? Or *Miriam*, meaning "bitterness" or maybe "plump"? Or *Nabal*, meaning "fool"? Is it coincidence that people in the Bible seem to live up, or down, to their names?

When it comes to naming children in the twenty-first century, modern-day parents often focus on how lyrical, trendy, or unique a name is. What a name means is considered relatively unimportant. Then, of course, some modern-day parents (especially those in the celebrity spotlight) bestow names on their children that seem more appropriate for a family pet. How about Apple, thanks to Gwyneth Paltrow and Chris Martin? Satchel? That one's courtesy of Mia Farrow and Woody Allen. Rumer? That's the brainchild of Demi Moore and Bruce Willis. How would you like to have a name such as Moon Unit, Dweezil, or Diva Muffin? Frank and Gail Zappa's creativity in naming their children seems to know no bounds.

My given name, Victoria, means "victory" or "victorious." This has always seemed a bit ironic to me, since my name was chosen as a last resort. My mother wanted to name me

Cathy Jean, a name she'd been fond of since she was a little girl. But apparently my father once dated a girl named Cathy and wasn't about to have a daughter whose name stirred up less-than-fond memories. So my parents began working their way through a baby name book. When they reached the last page, they still hadn't come up with a name they could agree on. "Want to look through it again?" my mom asked. My dad shook his head and said, "Why don't we just go with the last girl's name in the book?" And that's how I became Victoria Jean. Victoria was immediately shortened to Vicki, which has always sounded a bit like a breakfast cereal to me: Grab a bowl of Vicki Miller (or after marriage, Vicki Kuyper)! She never gets soggy in milk!

Nonetheless, I enjoy having a name associated with victory. In the same way that seeing purple wildflowers—whether tattooed or growing wild—reminds me of the beauty God has woven into me, hearing the sound of my name reminds me that I am victorious in this life (and the next!) because of what God has done for me. Even when I fall, victory remains close at hand. I'm not a failure. I'm a victor who's still in the heat of battle. Remembering this truth helps me persevere when life is hard.

My name isn't a magic word. It isn't a billboard that lets everyone know who I really am. It's merely a touchstone, something that helps point me back to the truth—back to what God says about me.

THE TRUE YOU

Whether the meaning of your given name is something you long to live up to or is as nonsensical as Diva Muffin, there are plenty of other names you and I carry with us every day. They are names we've picked up over the years. Some coincide with the truth, while others drown it out. Do you know what your names are?

Smart. Stupid. Cherished. Unlovable. Beautiful. Handsome. Unattractive. Talented. Ordinary. Insignificant. Powerful. Shy.

Popular. Outsider. Strong. Slacker. Sharp. Slow. Articulate. Loser. Precious. Worthless...the list goes on and on.

You may have picked up these names from others or have chosen to bestow them on yourself. Regardless of where they come from, these "secret" names are the building blocks of your identity. The problem is that building your identity on lies, even if they are mixed in with the truth, results in a faulty foundation. A foundation that isn't true to the schematics of a structure's original design will result in that structure's demise over time.

It's the same with you. You were designed to stand firm on a foundation of God's truth. This truth includes who you were created to be. If you try to live your life as someone you're not, whether consciously or unconsciously, something's eventually going to crack—and then crumble.

The good news is that this is often how we are first drawn into God's arms. For years we try to live life as though we are in charge of our own destiny. We keep telling ourselves that if we just work harder, make more money, lose weight, find the right spouse, land that big job, or whatever our own personal "if only" lie happens to be, everything will finally fall into place. *Then*, we assure ourselves, *we'll be happy and whole.* And along the way we do whatever is in our power to make these things happen—including trying to mold ourselves into the image of someone we feel would be most successful in achieving our goals.

One day (by God's grace), reality hits. Our charade crumbles, along with our well-laid plans. The truth hits us straight in the heart: God is God and we are not. What we do with this revelation changes the course of our lives, as well as our eternal destiny. Along with this revelation comes the opportunity to discover more about the identity of the great I Am. But that's not all. Just like Peter seeing himself for the first time through Jesus's eyes, we also catch a glimpse of our own true identity.

The word *true* is defined as "conforming with reality

or fact, genuine not pretend, insincere or artificial." It also means to be "perfectly in tune." We can't sing in perfect tune with a song we've never heard before or have even seen the sheet music to. To live out the truth of who God created us to be, we need to hear that truth firsthand. Simply listening to our hearts or trying to reason things out in our brains isn't the answer. Our emotional hearts and limited brains are not reliable soloists when it comes to carrying God's tune of truth about who you and I really are. We have to go to the Source of the song itself.

One of the best arenas to hear God's voice is found in Scripture. God's Word is filled with insights into the true you— the masterpiece God created you to be. Throughout the Bible, you'll find names, as well as God-given attributes and personal promises, that you have in common with every child of God. I've already mentioned that you're a bona fide masterpiece (Ephesians 2:10 NLT), but God doesn't stop there. You're a temple (1 Corinthians 6:19), a shining star (Philippians 2:15–16), salt (Matthew 6:13), and light (Matthew 6:14). You're a vital part of Christ's body, the church (1 Corinthians 12:26–27). You're a letter that tells the world about God (2 Corinthians 3:2). You're a priest (1 Peter 2:5) and a servant (Matthew 23:11), no longer a slave, but God's own child (Galatians 4:7). You're a treasured possession (Deuteronomy 7:6), who, without God's life-giving breath, is nothing more than dust (Psalm 103:13–14).

There is so much more truth about you and me to be sung! These are just a few bars to get us started. But we can't be content to be hearers of the truth. It's time to become doers; it's time to learn to sing along with God by living out who we were created to be. Just remember, it takes time and practice for a singer or musician to be perfectly in tune. Similarly, we need to repeat what we've heard in Scripture, and through the still, small voice of God's Spirit, over and over again. (Remember the importance of repetition for cementing something in our brains?) Then after awhile, we find we're no longer thinking about individual notes of truth. Singing in concert with who we were created to be begins to come as naturally as breathing. It doesn't matter if we're tone deaf or a natural-born diva muffin, this is one tune we were created to master.

You...the Tattoo

On occasion, we may still forget the truth about who we are and who God is. We may get distracted, deceived, or simply stage a rebellion. Yet God remains true. He never, ever forgets us. In Isaiah 49:14–16, God's children (Zion) cry, *"The Lord has forsaken me, the Lord has forgotten me."* But God replies, *"Can a mother forget the baby at her breast and have no compassion on the child she has borne? Though she may forget, I will not forget you! See, I have engraved you on the palms of my hands; your walls are ever before me."*

As is to be expected by big God, small brain Bible commentators (in other words, by any teachers, preachers, or scholars who happen to be part of the human race) there is disagreement over what being *engraved* on the palms of God's hands may really mean. Some believe God is alluding to tying a string around His finger to remind Him of His children and their true home in Jerusalem. Others link this verse to the custom of wearing a signet ring or locket as a way of remembering someone dear to one's heart.

I, however, find myself siding with the tattoo camp. (No big surprise there!) It seems there was a rather obscure Jewish custom where some of God's people made marks or punctured small holes on their hands or arms. This "tattooed" pattern represented Jerusalem or the Temple. The mark served as a touchstone, a reminder of what was really important—the city of God, where God's house and His presence dwelled.

Today, we are God's temple. Zion incarnate. That makes *us* the image tattooed on the palms of God's hands. (Metaphorically speaking, of course.) Like a burly guy with *Mom* inked on his arm, the almighty God has my name—and yours—tattooed on His palm. Every time He reaches out His hand, what does God see? His kids. He's reminded of how much He loves us. How much we need Him. How we'll all be together soon. It brings to mind what's important, what's eternal, what's true.

Though God's perfect memory never really needs jogging, the image of Him using a tattoo touchstone to bring us to mind can become a touchstone for us. If we wish, it can become a mental snapshot of His faithfulness. But scriptural metaphor can only take us so far when it comes to drawing our hearts and minds nearer to an invisible God. That's why God went beyond metaphor, beyond words, beyond what our wildest imaginations could have ever dreamed up to send us the ultimate Touchstone: our precious Savior, God's Son, Jesus Christ.

THE GOD OF OUR FIVE SENSES

We've talked about how difficult it is to connect with, and set our minds on, a God we can't see, hear, or hold. Someone we can't build a relationship with in the usual way. But that hasn't always been the case. Two thousand years ago God made a guest appearance here on earth. The infinite God wrapped Himself in finite flesh and walked the Judean countryside, teaching, healing, eating, sleeping, and relating to people in a way our human brains can comprehend.

Frankly, it makes me feel a little left out—like I was born two millennia too late. If only I'd been able to walk in the steps of His disciples, to see Lazarus rise from the dead, to hear the Sermon on the Mount firsthand, to have Jesus look me in the eye when I asked Him a question, imagine how much stronger my "little brain" faith would be.

Or not.

Even with God in their midst, not everyone Jesus met comprehended what was going on. The religious leaders, those who supposedly knew God's Word inside and out, were some of Jesus's biggest skeptics. In His own hometown, Jesus "did not do many miracles there because of their lack of faith" (Matthew 13:58). And even after spending three years by Jesus' side, Judas still loved money more than the Messiah.

All we have to do is read the Gospels to see that the big God, small brain dilemma seems to be just as much a problem with a visible God as with an invisible one. Seeing is not always synonymous with believing. That's why Jesus, God in the flesh, frequently used metaphors to help make things above more mentally accessible to folks below.

In Matthew 13:10, as paraphrased in *The Message*, the disciples ask Jesus why He tells stories. He replies this way:

> *"You've been given insight into God's kingdom. You know how it works. Not everybody has this gift, this insight; it hasn't been given to them. Whenever someone has a ready heart for this, the insights and understandings flow freely. But if there is no readiness, any trace of receptivity soon disappears. That's why I tell stories: to create readiness, to nudge the people toward receptive insight. In their present state they can stare till doomsday and not see it, listen till they're blue in the face and not get it."*
> —Matthew 13:10 (*The Message*)

A ready heart, that's what Jesus said was the key to getting a mental clue. Why do you think John the Baptist knew who Jesus was when He saw Him at the Jordan River? I believe it's because John was diligently searching for Him. Not just on the day Jesus arrived, but every day. Everything John did up to the day of Jesus's baptism was done to prepare the way for a Messiah John knew would come. Every day John kept his eyes open—and his heart ready.

If we long for insight into God's kingdom, we can take a lesson from John. We can do our part to nurture a ready heart. All the touchstones in the world won't help point us toward God if our hearts, and minds, aren't readily seeking what's of eternal worth.

WHAT—OR WHO—IS TRUTH?

A heart that is readily seeking the truth is a heart that is ultimately seeking Jesus. Remember how important names were in the ancient Jewish culture? One of the names Jesus used in reference to Himself was *the Truth* (John 14:6). In Jesus, infinite truth was made tangible, even if it was only for some 30-odd years. But by reading the Gospels, by letting our minds rest on the truth revealed through the parables and eyewitness accounts, we can walk side-by-side with a tangible Savior. We can watch Him lift a small child lovingly onto His lap in blessing. We can hear the compassionate strength in His voice as He tells a woman caught in the act of adultery to *"go and sin no more."* In our mind's eye, we can wash Jesus's feet with our tears in worship. We can peer into an empty tomb and rejoice, knowing that our once visible Savior will be seen again one day.

The truth as it is revealed in Christ is our ultimate touchstone. When our brains are squirming with questions, when the whys and hows and whens of things above send mental tremors through our faith, we can choose to cling firmly to the "Who" we've come to know. We can focus on who God is...the way, the truth and the life. Our wonderful Counselor. Our sacrificial Lamb. Our Mighty Warrior, Compassionate King, and Sovereign Lord.

When we focus on who God is, the truth of who we are seems to slide more easily into its proper place. We remember that no matter what the world says about us, we are beautiful. We are loved. We are victors. What we do and say matters in the eternal scheme of things. But truth also reminds us that if God is God, then we most assuredly are not. We remain mere mortals. Flawed, but forgiven. Loved, but limited. Servants, not "saviors" in a broken world. Holding on to this truth truly sets us free to be who God created us to be. No more. No less.

Deep "C" Fishing

1. Reread Matthew 13:10 as quoted from *The Message* on page 62 in this chapter.

• How can we nurture a ready heart?

• What is something you can do to help open your eyes a little wider to seeing God as an integral part of your everyday life?

Matthew, Mark, Luke & John

• Read through the Gospels as if this were the first time you've ever seen or heard them. (Reading a translation or paraphrased version of the Bible that's new to you can be helpful.) Read slowly and prayerfully, putting yourself in the sandals of the people Jesus meets. Share any new insights you gain into God's character—and into your own—with a friend or record them in your journal.

2. Revelation 2:17 (TNIV) says: *"Whoever has ears, let them hear what the Spirit says to the churches. To those who are victorious, I will give…each of them a white stone with a new name written on it, known only to the one who receives it."*

- Even though you won't know your new name (given to you on a touchstone, no less!) until heaven, are there any nicknames (like my Wildflower or Victorious) you believe God has whispered to you? SURVIVOR

- Are there any names you feel are ingrained in your brain that are lies, instead of God's truth? If so, start a list of Scripture verses that tell the truth about who you are. Ask God to provide firsthand experiences, along with verses of Scripture, to help replace any lies you may be holding on to about your true identity.

  Unloved, Unnoticable, undeserving

  Matthew 5:11   Matthew 6:25-34

  matthew 7:7

- Find a touchstone that reminds you of how God sees you. Whenever any of your old insecurities or misperceptions about yourself rear their ugly, untruthful heads, use your touchstone as a reminder of God's truth—and a reminder to go to God in prayer, asking Him to help you uncover what caused this lie to be resurrected in the first place.

- What effect does keeping close at hand the truth about who we are and who God is—have on pride and humility? Consider God's words as voiced in Psalm 50:21—*"You thought I was altogether like you"*—in light of your answer.

3. When Moses asked God his name (Exodus 3:14), God's reply was *"I AM WHO I AM."* The name I AM is derived from the Hebrew verb for "to be." When Jesus uses this same name to refer to Himself in John 8:58 *("I tell you the truth," Jesus answered, "before Abraham was born, I am!"),* the crowds tried to stone Him for blasphemy. Back then, the Jewish people might consider God's name so holy that they refused to speak it aloud. They were afraid they might unintentionally use God's name in a way that might dishonor Him. Knowing what you know about the importance of names in the Jewish culture, consider the following verses: Hebrews 13:8; Revelation 1:8; and Revelation 4:8.

- What can you tell about the essence of who God is from His name? onmipotent

- What other names, or metaphors, for God are especially significant in your life?

- Create a new touchstone by coming up with your own personal word picture for God. I've shared my slippery-fish metaphor, which not only says something about God but something about my own relationship with Him. What would be an accurate metaphor for your relationship?

CHAPTER FIVE

USING DOWNTIME
TO LIFT UP OUR MINDS

"Whatever is noble."
—Philippians 4:8

The handsome prince mounts his noble steed and turns toward the setting sun, ready to battle the evil wizard and rescue the beautiful princess..." So goes the basic outline for most fairy tales. You can swap out the evil wizard for a jealous queen, fire-breathing dragon, wicked witch, or even the princess's own personal bout with PMS, but the story line remains the same. The prince puts his own safety on the line by charging off to help fight someone else's battle. So why is it that the steed is usually the one that gets labeled noble?

Turn on any wildlife documentary and you're bound to hear something along those same lines: "The noble lion surveys the open savannah, searching for his next meal"; or "The noble grizzly lowers the wriggling salmon into his gaping jaws." When the word *noble* is used to describe the animal kingdom, it's a synonym for "impressive in appearance" or "free." But when it comes to setting our minds on *"whatever is noble"* in the context of Philippians 4:8, the animal kingdom simply doesn't have what it takes.

But we do. You and I were created in the image of nobility. And I don't mean that in terms of royalty or rank. By definition, someone who is noble has a strong moral fiber and exhibits qualities such as courage, generosity, and honor. This kind of character naturally invites reverence, respect, and esteem. Sounds pretty lofty. Maybe that's why in today's society *noble* is not a word that's often heard outside the realm of fairy tales and Animal Planet. But that doesn't mean chivalry is dead. It's not only alive and flourishing, but something worth setting our minds on more frequently than "once upon a time."

THAT'S ENTERTAINMENT!

If our goal is to set our minds on *"whatever is noble,"* taking a closer look at entertainment may seem rather counterintuitive. But I've found that how I choose to amuse myself during my free time can play a big role, or become a big roadblock, in fostering noble thoughts. If I believe Corinthians 10:31 really means what it says, then everything I do should be done *"for the glory of God."* That includes what I do with my downtime. I don't believe that verse mandates that I read Bible commentaries instead of a novel, watch a televangelist instead of the cooking channel, or turn off Evanescence and turn on a worship CD. But it does mean I need to be intentional about where I allow my brain to "go out and play."

Like our bodies, our brains need time to relax. Research suggests that after four hours of intense concentration, the brain needs a little R & R. If we don't take time for some shut-eye or mental relaxation at this point, it becomes more difficult for us to concentrate and stay focused. That's actually one positive reason why our minds wander. They are taking a self-imposed, much needed time-out. Studies show that on average, our minds take a little detour away from the task, or conversation at hand 30 to 40 percent of the time. During a brain-intensive task that takes focused concentration, such as reading, research suggests that our minds wander only 15 to 20 percent, according to Malcolm Ritter in the *Arizona Republic*. Perhaps that's why after four hours of concentration our brains crave a bit of relaxation. They need some time to roam free!

But a wandering brain is not always "out of the office." Another reason our brains wander is because they're searching our mental file folders trying to make new associations, trying to consolidate, trying to learn. By wandering off, they're actually working hard to ensure we remember something new.

But my brain has wandered from its original topic. Back to entertainment. When I am faced with a potential chunk of free time, my brain longs to wander far and wide. I want to forget about deadlines, pending bills, and interpersonal struggles. I want a pleasant distraction to lead me far away from the unavoidable stress of living in a fallen world. Books, movies, television, and music are often the roads I choose to take me away. But whether I choose to wander the high road or the low is up to me.

It's embarrassing to admit, but this topic makes me squirm. Though I struggle with consistently setting my mind on things above, I seem to have no problem letting it rest awhile on much lower surfaces, especially when I relax. Say, reruns of *The X-Files*. That's not to put *The X-Files* on some bottom rung of the moral entertainment ladder. For me, it usually ranks as more of a neutral, entertainment-for-entertainment's sake rung.

However, if the average American watches nearly 4 hours of television a day (as recent polls suggests we do), that means by the time I'm 50, I will have spent over eight full years, 24 hours a day, setting my mind on "the tube." Even if I am below the average when it comes to how many hours of television I watch a day, the number of TV hours I accumulate over my lifetime should still give me pause. That's quite a chunk of time to set my mind on entertaining myself. (And that doesn't include going to movies and theatrical productions, listening to music, playing games, reading books and magazines, or just hanging out doing "nothing." But to keep things simple, let's just stick to the TV right now.)

My television set does not turn itself on. I make a conscious decision to hit the power button on the remote and plop myself down in front of it for several hours every week. In contrast, how many hours a week do I make a conscious decision to set my mind on things above?

Although I do believe that television commercials have the potential to stir up ripples of discontent in our lives, I don't believe television in and of itself is intrinsically evil. As a matter of fact, I believe that even what I watch on TV can become a spiritual touchstone, if I choose to use it in a more "noble" fashion. Renowned broadcast journalist Edward R. Murrow said, "This instrument can teach, it can illuminate; yes, and it can even inspire. But it can do so only to the extent that humans are determined to use it to those ends. Otherwise, it is nothing but wires and lights in a box."

Television is just a fancy electronic tool. How that tool is used is up to the person wielding the remote. It's true that there are plenty of things on the air that anyone with an eye on nobility should refuse to set their minds on at all. For me, these programs call to mind the floor of a long-neglected subway restroom that is littered with filth. I'm not about to set the purse I carry around with me every day down on that disgusting surface. If I'm careful where I set my purse, I should be even more careful where I set my brain!

When it comes to entertainment, choosing a suitable surface I can rest my brain on for awhile takes prayer, forethought, and resolve. Not only are my choices not black and white, but they are also going to differ from those around me—even from fellow Christ followers.

For me, one of the measuring sticks I use to determine what to watch, read, or listen to is *"whatever is noble."* Does it stir noble themes in me, themes of self-sacrifice and standing up for what's right in God's eyes? Does it draw me toward, and not away from, the moral center God has forged in my conscience and through His Word? Does it invite and attract me in a way God would look favorably on? Does it help move me forward toward maturing into the person God created me to be?

Not everything I entertain myself with consistently gets an A in every area. On occasion I choose to watch something just because I need a good laugh. If the humor I'm enjoying seems like something that God Himself might smile at, that's good enough for me. After all, God was the one who came up with the idea of laughter. I certainly wouldn't want one of His gifts to go to waste.

Also, when God created me He gave me a heart that responds deeply to a wide variety of artistic expressions. I'm continually inspired and refreshed by innovative creativity in others. However, there are limits to where I want someone else's creative work to take me and my thoughts. So, I read lots of reviews and ask for recommendations from friends whose opinions I trust. I try to choose how to best spend my entertainment time wisely.

But "art" can surprise you. Sometimes I walk out of a movie or change a TV channel midprogram. Sometimes I toss a highly recommended book in the trash. (I can't bring myself to put it in someone else's hands by donating or selling it.) Sometimes I catch myself singing lyrics to a song that goes against what my heart truly believes—and I turn off the radio. Then again, sometimes I don't. Sometimes I continue watching, reading, and listening. God and I are working on that.

But along the way, I've picked up a few valuable spiritual touchstones from the entertainment world, sometimes from seemingly unlikely sources. Movies like *The Color Purple*, *The Lord of the Rings*, and *Schindler's List* have awakened noble themes in me. Books like *The Kite Runner* by Khaled Hosseini, *The Secret Life of Bees* by Sue Monk Kidd, and *To Kill a Mockingbird* by Harper Lee corner me into asking myself,

"What would I do in this situation? Would my response be noble and above reproach in God's eyes? If not, how do I need to grow and change?" Songs such as "Unwritten" by Natasha Bedingfield, "Hold Your Head Up" by Argent, and "Beautiful" by Christina Aguilera encourage me to more boldly live out the truth of my God-designed self. And believe it or not, on occasion even *The X-Files* has challenged me to better understand why I *do* believe in God.

Does that mean that everything in these artistic expressions is good and pure and right? No. But what is noble in them lies at their core. God has placed the tuning fork of His Spirit in me that vibrates with the perfect pitch of nobility. I can tell when something is in tune with God, because what I'm seeing, hearing, or reading is resonating with that one note, even when certain elements of the story run in direct contrast to it. And God uses that noble note as a catalyst—a touchstone—to move my mind from a simple story or song on toward higher things.

The "R-Rated" Book that Changed My Life

There is one book I've read over and over again for the last 30 years that's filled with sex, violence, idolatry, and unadulterated evil. It's called the Bible—and if it made it to the big screen in its entirety, there is no way it would earn a G rating. Or even PG. Yet, Paul tells us in 2 Timothy 3:16–17 (TNIV), *"All Scripture is God-breathed and is useful for teaching, rebuking, correcting and training in righteousness, so that all God's people may be thoroughly equipped for every good work."*

All Scripture, even those storylines we'd declare morally bankrupt in any other context, was given to us by God through human hands to provide us with what we need to live a life pleasing to Him. Sounds like pretty noble stuff to me. God trusted we'd be able to sort the good from the evil, the wise from the foolish, the noble from the ignoble as we read our way through the history of the world via the pages of His Word.

From beginning to end, God doesn't whitewash the lives

of His own handpicked "heroes," people like Abraham, Moses, David, and Peter. Right alongside their victories, God records their moral meltdowns and crises of faith. I believe that's one reason why the Bible continues to feel relevant to us today. Every generation can relate to people who fail, who doubt, who blow it, even when they really want to do what's noble and right—people who forget who God is and what He's done in the past; people who've experienced God's slippery fish–like immensity.

Though every word of Scripture is a God-given touchstone, the historical books of the Old Testament, the Gospels, and the Book of Acts can be particularly helpful when it comes to setting our minds on whatever is noble. These books are different from the tenets, precepts, and prophecies that encourage and instruct us throughout the remainder of Scripture. They *show* us instead of just *tell* us what kind of life invites reverence, respect, and esteem—and what kind of life does not.

Historical books are the Bible's action films, tragedies, comedies, and love stories. Some of them even read like fairy tales. (Though the Song of Solomon is classified more as poetic literature than a historical book, it's an adult fairy tale if ever I've read one!) Talk about entertainment with a noble purpose...the Bible's got it all!

Which then begs the question: Why do we so rarely pick up the Bible and read it in our so-called free time? Now, maybe I'm projecting my own personal habits, or lack thereof, too much upon you. Maybe you read Scripture at stoplights and spend your three-day weekends cuddled up under a quilt with a refrigerator-sized King James. But in my experience, most Christians I talk to struggle to make time to read the Bible.

I am a book person. I love to read. And I can truthfully say that I love to read God's Word. Almost every morning I spend some time reading Scripture and talking to God in prayer. Yet, when I come face-to-face with a lazy Saturday afternoon or an evening when there's nothing worth watching on TV, why doesn't it ever cross my mind to pick up the Bible and read for awhile? Does reading God's own words not feel like a big enough "treat"? Do I consider the activity too taxing for a relaxing brain?

Personally, I think my answer is buried in the questions above. I guess I look at the Bible the same way I do vegetables. I know I need veggies to stay healthy and I've even tried to develop a taste for them over time. But when I'm craving a treat, I'll choose a hunk of cheesecake over a hunk of broccoli every time.

That choice is more than just a matter of taste. It's a matter of perspective. As a kid, "treating myself" was synonymous with sugar. Cake, ice cream, cookies, candy, doughnuts, soda...those were treats. If any food was "healthy" for me, that automatically eliminated it from the "treat" category.

As an adult, I've begun to intentionally forge some new associations in my mind. A juicy peach, a piece of grilled salmon with mango chipotle salsa, and yes, even a green salad, fresh string beans, or herbed asparagus spears can satisfy me as much, or even more, than a caloric dessert. The trick is to get my brain to reclassify these foods into the "treat" category. Some days it clicks. Some days I reach for the Oreos.

The same logic holds for the way I view God's Word. I know I should *"taste and see that the* LORD *is good"* (Psalm 34:8) by munching on His Word. I know reading Scripture is a spiritually healthy habit. And I also know that the more I read, the hungrier I get for what God has to teach me. Now, I just need to make some new associations. I need to retrain my brain to recognize that reading God's Word is more than a minimum daily requirement I should fill. It can also be a treat.

Recalibrating my spiritual taste buds won't happen overnight. (It certainly hasn't happened that way with my physical taste buds.) But that doesn't mean it can't be done. All it takes is some desire, forethought, and self-discipline.

The Bible is an all-around incomparable gift from God. It

also serves as a uniquely inspired touchstone to things above. In this chapter we're choosing to focus on whatever is noble, but I will mention how the Bible can be used as a touchstone over and over again throughout this book. Finding new ways to incorporate Scripture into our lives is like getting a two-for-one deal. As we use it to help steer our minds more toward what is true or noble or any of the adjectives the Apostle Paul uses in Philippians 4:8, we acquire more of a taste for God's Word. The more we crave Scripture, the more we're inclined to invest our time and energy into actively fishing for the great I Am.

My taste for God's Word at this stage in my life is much greater than it was 10 or 20 years ago. Hopefully before the next decade goes by, I'll find myself reaching for the Bible at least as often as I do the TV remote. After all, in my free time I'm usually seeking refreshment and rejuvenation. Personally, I find both by exploring unfamiliar territory.

The people I meet in the Bible transport me across time, continents, and cultures. Their stories lead me to foreign lands, life situations, and ways of thinking. Their victories and downfalls inspire me to superimpose my life on theirs, to try on their nobility—or treachery—for size. As I size up my own life, I see where God's image is shining through and where it is obscured by sin or weakness. I see where nobility lies and where it is absent.

As I get better acquainted with the individuals that make up my spiritual family tree, I am challenged to consider my own place among the heroes of faith as touched upon in Hebrews 11. If my life were recorded within these pages, how would it read? What would the moral of my story be? Would reading about me lead others to set their minds on what is noble?

Sobering questions, indeed...and it's questions like these that inspire me to keep a special touchstone tucked inside the cover of my Bible. It's a reminder of both my true identity and of the noble life I was created to lead.

Passport to Nobility

Inside the red leather cover of my Bible, I keep a photocopy of my passport. Sure, it's handy to have an extra copy when I travel outside the country, in case my real passport winds up in "enemy" hands—or more likely, is forgotten on the back of a toilet tank in a foreign airport. But that's only one reason why I keep a passport photo (one that makes me look like an aging rock star in rehab) so close at hand. The most important reason is that over the years my passport has become a spiritual touchstone. Just catching sight of it helps me set my mind on what is noble and true.

I travel. A lot. And sometimes I find myself in a country that is suspicious of outsiders. It may even be a place where the word *American is* a swear word. But I *am* an American. All anyone has to do is look at my passport to verify that fact. And regardless of how others may view me because of my nationality, I'm proud of what America stands for.

When I travel, I'm very aware that I represent more than just myself. I also represent the United States. I'm an ambassador dressed in tourist's clothing. So I do my best to act in a way that reflects well on my country. I study up on, and respect, the customs of the country I'm visiting. I try to learn at least a few words of the local language. I strive to be courteous, attentive, and genuine with everyone I interact with. And I pray that I will demonstrate God's love in ways that reach beyond barriers of language, culture, or preconceived prejudice.

That's because I am more than just an American citizen. According to Philippians 3:20, I am also a citizen of heaven. Every time I catch sight of the passport in my Bible I'm reminded of this dual citizenship. I may have an "endless summer" home awaiting me in heaven, but while I'm here on earth, I'm an ambassador of God's kingdom to those around me. And some days, even America can feel like a very foreign land.

My passport reminds me that my faith in God may label me a foreigner in the eyes of some people I meet today. They may have preconceived notions about who I am, what I believe, and how my faith plays itself out in my life. So I need to offer those around me the same courtesy I do any time I travel in a foreign country—I need to be aware of widespread customs so I can better understand what the "locals" believe to be acceptable and why. I try to speak their language, avoiding the use of the Christian catchphrases and colloquialisms that are so common within the evangelical church. And I endeavor to be courteous, attentive, and genuine, in accordance with 1 Peter 3:15: *"Always be prepared to give an answer to everyone who asks you to give the reasons for the hope that you have. But do this with gentleness and respect."*

Do I always succeed? Nope. I often fumble in foreign lands, those both literal and spiritual. I trip over customs and get tongue-tied when conversations head to unfamiliar territory. But that doesn't stop me from traveling, from venturing out of my safe little cocoon of the familiar. What good would a passport do for me if I never left home?

The travel-worn copy of my passport is a touchstone that helps set my mind on living a noble life. The Greek word *semnós*, which is translated into English as "noble," is defined in *The Complete Word Study Dictionary* as "not only earthly dignity, but that which is derived from a higher citizenship, a heavenly one, which is the possession of all believers. There lies something of majestic and awe-inspiring qualities in *semnós* which does not repel but rather invites and attracts."

A noble act invites and attracts. Noble men and women do the same. If I want to be an "attractive" woman, the secret isn't found in toning my body, plumping up my hormone-deprived lips, or finding an outfit that accents my curves (while concealing my addiction to cheesecake). The secret is found in living a noble life. Setting my mind on whatever is noble is a start, but it's only a first step. If my noble thoughts don't give birth to noble actions, they are nothing more than spiritually stillborn fantasies.

From Fairy Tale to Raw Reality

Pam Cope was just a woman on vacation when her husband picked up a copy of the *New York Times* and commented, "You have to read the front page." The cover photo communicated almost as much as the feature article itself. The image captured the haunted expression of a six-year-old boy sold by his parents into slave labor in Ghana's fishing industry. In the article, journalist Sharon LaFraniere reported how children as young as age four worked 14-hour days, 7 days a week, beginning long before dawn. Although not all of the children knew how to swim when they arrived, they had to learn quickly to survive. Many of them spent their days diving into frigid waters to raise fishing nets. Most were beaten and given little to eat. Some drowned. Some simply shut down emotionally and did what they needed to do to survive.

When Pam read that article, she did more than think noble thoughts. She took action. She found a way to rescue seven children from slavery in Ghana, including Mark, the child in the *Times* photo. And she didn't stop there. She began Touch a Life Ministries and went to work rescuing even more children in Ghana, as well as helping children in Vietnam and Cambodia.

How do I know this? I watched *Oprah*. Talk shows are not usually high on my list of chosen entertainment, but this topic caught my eye. What I heard captured my heart.

True life stories, those that reveal situations that cry out for a noble response (like child slavery in Ghana) or that tell the story of how one person made a positive difference in the world (like Pam Cope), can become powerful spiritual touchstones in our lives. Documentaries, talk shows, biographies, and even the daily news can help turn our thoughts toward things above by opening our eyes to how different life is "here below."

But as I said, noble thoughts are worth nothing if they do not lead to noble acts. Who cares if Prince Charming thought about risking his life to save the princess, but chose to stay home and watch reruns of *American Idol* instead?

It's true that we cannot save the world. That's God's job. But, God does ask us to be His co-workers in certain situations. Our hearts are not large enough, or strong enough, to battle every injustice we become aware of, especially in this age of nonstop, worldwide media coverage. But we can do something. The where, when, and what of that action is between God and us as individuals. It doesn't matter whether our action goes unnoticed or whether it lands us a guest appearance on *Oprah*. What matters is we helped bring things above down to God's world below.

One way I can do that is through prayer. When I read the newspaper every morning, I don't regard it simply as a source of information. I view it as a potential touchstone. As I skim the headlines, some stories cry out for more help than human hands can offer. Others invite someone to step up and do something noble. Still others tell the stories of those who did step up, of those who became everyday heroes. I find my head and heart filling with prayers...for countries and individuals, for healing and hope, for wisdom for world leaders, for people to see God in the midst of chaos, and sometimes simply for Jesus's return.

Prayer is not a little thing. It unleashes the power of a mighty hand. But God, and His call to nobility, won't let me stay on my knees forever. Sometimes God calls me to become the answer to a prayer I have prayed. Prayers such as these have drawn people to become missionaries, social workers, doctors, ministers, police officers, and even politicians.

But not everyone is destined for a full-time career or a dramatic life change, fueled by noble thoughts and actions. Someone has to harvest the crops we need to survive. Someone has to handle the paperwork necessary to purchase a home. Someone has to fix the plumbing when it malfunctions, manage the trash we dispose of, and write the computer software necessary to keep the communications satellites we rely on from crashing into convenience stores. Not being in a service or ministry-oriented job doesn't mean that the rest of us don't have the opportunity to lead a noble life—to live a hero's life.

CALLING ALL HEROES: CAPE OPTIONAL

The more we set our minds on whatever is noble, the more job openings we'll notice for everyday heroes. We'll find them posted on the disabled car of a stranger, on the door of a neighbor in need, on the faces of family and friends. The "princess" we rescue may be a mom in need of an afternoon out while we watch her kids. The "dragon" we slay may be the loneliness that haunts an elderly acquaintance when we take time to visit a nursing home. The "noble steed" we ride may be a sacrificial check that finds its way from our tight budget to a refugee camp on the other side of the world. The "kingdom" we fight for is God's—a kingdom Jesus said can be found within you and me (Luke 17:21).

Setting our thoughts on noble things may be a safe place to visit every once in awhile, but it's a dangerous place to set up camp for any length of time. As a catchy slogan used a few years back by CBA (the Christian Booksellers Association) reminds us, "What goes into the mind comes out in a life." Consistently setting our minds on whatever is noble will challenge us to put feet on our faith and take action. It will push us closer toward the brink of self-sacrifice, generosity, and love. It will interfere with our schedules, push us outside our comfort zones, and sometimes break our hearts. It will expose the kingdom within us.

Once the nobility of that kingdom is out in the open the most amazing things can happen. We may find ourselves choosing to use more of our downtime to lift others up. In turn, our noble acts may become touchstones that inspire others to act, triggering a landslide of compassion.

Just ask Jason Russell, Bobby Bailey, and Laren Poole. These 20-something filmmakers from California headed to Africa in the spring of 2003 for a little adventure in filmmaking. Little did they know that the story God would connect them with would change the course of their lives—and become a touchstone used to inspire others around the world toward noble action.

When these three young men found themselves stranded in northern Uganda, they witnessed firsthand the plight of the "night commuters." For the last 20 years, the Sudan has been torn apart by a civil war, fought in part by children forced to become soldiers. Children as young as eight years old are often kidnapped by a group that calls itself the Lord's Resistance Army (LRA) and forced to witness and commit almost unimaginable atrocities. Every evening thousands of children in the Sudan leave their homes to walk, sometimes for hours, to the relative safety of a larger town to sleep. These night commuters sleep en masse in public places and then wake early to begin their long walk home.

Invisible Children: Rough Cut, the documentary made by Russell, Bailey, and Poole, tells much more of this story, and their Web site at www.invisiblechildren.com explains the change that has begun to take place since the film's debut. The film was a touchstone for me, a heart's cry to take personal action in a story where heroes are desperately needed. I pulled out my checkbook (one valid response to a noble cause) and prepared for the usual "love offering." Imagine my surprise when I was offered a touchstone in return.

A bracelet handmade in Uganda and a DVD telling one child's personal story from his or her war-torn childhood in the Sudan comes as a gift for every $20 donation. That gave me an idea. My husband and I have many night commuters of our own, people who journey to our guest room in need of a safe haven. (You'll read more about our Heart Rock Café and Oasis in chap. 12.) But our visitors sleep on a pillow-top mattress instead of a cold concrete floor.

From that day on, those who sleep under our roof find a touchstone on their pillow—a bracelet and DVD from the nonprofit organization Invisible Children. These simple gifts have the power to educate and inspire our guests, while at the same time providing jobs and income to the people of Sudan. They are a touchstone to help myself and others set our minds on whatever is noble. And with God's help, what goes into our minds will come out in our lives.

Deep "C" Fishing

1. Put modesty aside for a moment and take an honest look at what part nobility plays in your life and in your thoughts.

• Imagine for a moment that you are listed along with other heroes of the faith in Hebrews 11. Write a "verse" describing how your noble actions have given evidence of your faith in God.

• What "hero" in Hebrews 11 most inspires your thoughts toward whatever is noble? Why?

• Who is a modern-day hero whose actions inspire you? How would you like to be more of a hero in your daily life? Is there any specific action you need to take?

2. First Corinthians 10:23 tells us: *"'Everything is permissible'— but not everything is beneficial. 'Everything is permissible'— but not everything is constructive."*

- When it comes to entertainment and how we spend our downtime, what practical insights can we gain from the verse above?

- What is your favorite television show? What's appealing about it to you? Does it lead your thoughts toward noble ground?

- What personal entertainment touchstones have you gathered over the years. Think about any genre—film, TV, DVDs, music CDs, Web sites or online discussions you regularly participate in, or others. How have they inspired or challenged you? Have they changed you in any way?

3. From the outside, the Bible may look like just another book on the shelf, but it differs from anything else we've ever read. Hebrews 4:12 (NKJV) says: "*The word of God is living and powerful, and sharper than any two-edged sword, piercing even to the division of soul and spirit, and of joints and marrow, and is a discerner of the thoughts and intents of the heart.*" In the NLT, the end of the verse reads: "*It exposes our innermost thoughts and desires.*"

- How do you view the Bible? Do you believe it's wholly God's words? Literal? Some figurative? Fact mixed with fiction? Inerrant? Do you believe it's "living"? If so, how?

- What part does the Bible play in your life and your thoughts? Is there any change you'd like to see in its importance to you?

- Has a specific Scripture been a touchstone for you in the past? How?

- Read more about the hero from Hebrews you selected in question 1, keeping your mind focused on whatever is noble. Then, mentally put yourself in this hero's sandals for awhile. What would you do differently? What can he or she teach you about God, faith, and being human?

CHAPTER SIX

HANGING ON TO
THE RIGHT STUFF

"Whatever is right."
—Philippians 4:8

From floods, plagues, war, death, fire, and brimstone to forgiveness, grace, love, life, and turning the other cheek.... At first glance, the Old Testament Yahweh and New Testament Jesus seem to paint conflicting pictures of God's preferred approach to dealing with right and wrong. Thinking the Almighty goes from fierce Warrior to humble Servant in that turn of a page between Malachi and Matthew can be a slippery-fish moment, one that brings to mind words like *bipolar.* Or it can simply lead us back to the "big God, small brain" dilemma.

But if we are going to let our minds rest for awhile on *"whatever is right,"* chances are our thoughts are going to have to grapple with just this kind of stuff: right and wrong, good and evil, sin and sacrifice, grace and punishment, love and the lack thereof. This can be fodder for a gripping theological debate or a downright divisive dispute. Or we can view it as an opportunity to search for touchstones that will help us better align our hearts and our heads—as well as our actions—with our wholly righteous God.

GOD'S TOP TEN

As a kid attending Catholic Church, I used to lie during confession. Once a month for about two years after my first communion (up to the point when my family stopped going to church altogether) I would fidget anxiously in the pitch-black, phone booth–sized confessional as I waited to say, "Bless me Father, for I have sinned. It has been one month since my last confession. These are my sins . . ." Then I would recite something like this: "I hit my sister two times, said mean words four times, took a cookie from the kitchen when I wasn't supposed to, and lied twice." Of course, I didn't bother to mention that the list I just "confessed" was a lie.

I lied in confession because I couldn't think of anything I'd done wrong. However, I was required to go to confession every month and I knew I'd have to say, "I have sinned." So, I had to come up with something. I was also aware that chances were pretty good that I'd actually committed some of the offenses on my fake list over the past month. I just didn't remember them—or didn't want to take the time to reflect long enough to call them to mind.

I had learned the Ten Commandments in catechism, but frankly, when I laid my elementary school–aged life up against them I really didn't see any major infractions. I hadn't killed anyone or used God's name as a curse word. I had no true understanding of what it meant to "covet," but I felt pretty certain I wasn't doing it to my next-door neighbor's wife or his lawn mower, barbecue grill, or anything else he claimed as his own. After all, I was generally obedient, did well in school, and was an all-around good kid. That's not because I had a heart of gold, but because I didn't see any real benefit to doing what I understood to be wrong. In addition, my father ruled our house with an iron fist, which wielded a leather belt.

One reason I did what was right was because I was afraid to do anything but.

When I read the Old Testament, I wonder if the Israelites saw themselves much in the same light as I saw myself in elementary school—all-around good kids trying to live up to the expectations of an iron-fisted Almighty. (From what I can glean from Scripture, God apparently had a different take on the situation.) In the Israelites' defense, they didn't receive God's Top Ten List until after they'd tromped around the desert for awhile. They could claim it wasn't fair to be held responsible for following rules they didn't know about. Of course, Moses had previously shared God's words with them aloud, but you and I know how forgetful we humans tend to be. So, God decided His kids needed a touchstone to help them discern what was right.

And what a touchstone it was—a succinct, easy to memorize list of God's Top Ten Commands, personally inscribed on stone tablets by the metaphorical finger of the eternal I Am. Along with the Top Ten, God also gave the Israelites rules for dealing with issues like restitution, sacrifices, and social justice. Unfortunately, the first time God tried to give His children this touchstone, they were so busy breaking the as-yet-unread commands that God's courier (Moses) angrily threw the stone tablets to the ground, smashing them to bits. Take two. New tablets, same rules.

God encouraged His people to do more than just read what He'd written. He told them to

"Fix these words of mine in your hearts and minds; tie them as symbols on your hands and bind them on your foreheads. Teach them to your children, talking about them when you sit at home and when you walk along the road, when you lie down and when you get up. Write them on the doorframes of your houses and on your gates."
—Deuteronomy 11:18–20

The Israelites took God's words very literally and created touchstones to help remind them to do what He asked. To this day, some Orthodox and conservative Jewish males wear phylacteries on their forehead or arm during morning prayers. These black leather boxes hold portions of Scripture, including the one quoted above. And in Jewish homes, a *mezuzah* (a container holding the same portions of Scripture as the phylacteries) is often affixed to one or more of the doorframes.

Unfortunately, though God's people may have bound His words to their biceps, binding them to their hearts and minds was another matter. Even knowing what was right couldn't assure that God's people would act on what they knew. As Romans 3:20 (NLT) reminds us, *"No one can ever be made right in God's sight by doing what his law commands. For the more we know God's law, the clearer it becomes that we aren't obeying it."*

What was true for the Israelites remains true for each one of us today. The more we set our minds on what is right, the more aware we become of how far we are from it.

From "Thou Shalt Not" to "You Shall"

So, that's the bad news. But Jesus is a bearer of good news. And this good news is not reserved solely for the New Testament but echoes powerfully throughout the Old. We hear it in Jeremiah 31:31: *"'A time is coming,' declares the Lord, 'when I will make a new covenant with the house of Israel.'"* God goes on to say, *"I will put my law in their minds and write it on their hearts"* (v. 33). The writer of Hebrews quotes this same passage (8:7–12) when speaking about the New Covenant Jesus' sacrifice has sealed for us. With the help of the Holy Spirit, it's out with the stone tablets and in with the cerebral cortex.

That doesn't mean that in these New Testament/New Covenant times, that God's Top Ten is obsolete. Jesus makes that point very clear in His Sermon on the Mount. In Matthew, chapter 5, Jesus emphasizes that He isn't abolishing the Law, but fulfilling it to a greater depth than it's ever been fulfilled before. And for all of those "good kids" like me, who feel as though we pretty much have it all together, Jesus's words expose us for who we really are. Jesus said this:

> *"You have heard that the law of Moses says, 'Do not murder. If you commit murder, you are subject to judgment.' But I say, if you are angry with someone, you are subject to judgment! If you call someone an idiot, you are in danger of being brought before the high council. And if you curse someone, you are in danger of the fires of hell....You have heard that the law of Moses says, 'Do not commit adultery.' But I say, anyone who even looks at a woman with lust in his eye has already committed adultery with her in his heart."*
> —Matthew 5:21–22, 27–28 (NLT)

Yikes. If I were sitting on that hillside at Jesus's feet the day He spoke these words, I know that at this point I would not have been able to look Him in the eye. Murderer. Adulterer. Idolater—He was talking about me. The so-called good kid. Whatever confidence I had in my own goodness, or superiority I'd previously felt to those whose lives didn't outwardly appear to line up as closely with Scripture as I felt mine did, would have vanished. I would have been painfully aware that Jesus saw through my "right stuff" façade. And, at that moment, I would certainly have seen through it as well.

In reality, you and I *are* sitting on that hillside. We're at Jesus's feet every time we open the Bible to read Scripture or open our hearts to pray—and every time we choose to set our minds on things above. We can don our WWJD bracelets as a touchstone to remind us to ask ourselves what Jesus would do in a given situation. But the truth is that doing what is right goes much deeper than that. What we really need to ask ourselves is "What would Jesus think?"

Doing what's right is both an inside and an outside job. The more we ponder the law God has written on our hearts and minds—as well as in Scripture—the more we'll recognize "right" when we see it and the less we'll be thrown off track by the counterfeit "good enough" that is so often an acceptable measure in our world.

However, if we're honest with ourselves, choosing to set our minds on God's law doesn't sound very inviting. For many of us, enthusiastically joining in with the psalmist who says, *"Oh, how I love your law! I meditate on it all day long"* (Psalm 119:97) may seem like a bit of a stretch, even if we really love the Lord. That's because meditating on God's law can bring to mind tedious Jewish rules, bizarre animal sacrifices, heady theology, and a strict list of *"Thou shalt nots."* Or perhaps it stirs up a picture of musty law libraries, people in suits, hushed courtrooms, and the sharp rap of a judge's gavel. We don't automatically connect with what seems like lifeless law. We're moved by story, creativity, and compassion. What we long for is relationship, not statutes. And leave it to God to offer us exactly what we long for.

If we continue reading after the Sermon on the Mount in the Book of Matthew, we'll witness Jesus's encounter with a Pharisee, an expert in the Law. This man asks Jesus, *"Teacher, which is the greatest commandment in the Law?"* Jesus replies: *"'Love the Lord your God with all your heart and with all your soul and with all your mind.' This is the first and greatest commandment. And the second is like it: 'Love your neighbor as yourself.' All the Law and the Prophets hang on these two commandments"* (Matthew 22:36–40).

From Ten Commandments to two, from stone tablets to our frontal lobes...once more God assists us in our big God, small brain dilemma. "You must love God and love people" is certainly short and catchy enough that we can set our minds on it more easily than on a long list of *"thou shalt nots."* And let's face it, *love* sounds so much more inviting and approachable than *Law*.

But if what is right is intrinsically tied to loving God and loving others, what does that really look like? How does it play out in our minds? In our hearts? In our lives? At the risk of sounding rather obtuse, what, exactly, is love?

All We Need Is Love—Right?

Go ahead. Try to define love in ten words or less. Not so easy, is it? And if our picture of love is drawn from movies, TV sitcoms, or romance novels—not to mention relationships with imperfect people—the definition of love we carry with us can become as variable (and subjective) as we are. I think most people would agree that true love is mankind's deepest longing and purest motivation. But after that, things get a bit fuzzy.

We can see and feel the effects of being in love or of someone else's loving action toward us. But love itself is rather elusive. It has no physical form. We can't hold it in our hands or catch sight of it out of the corner of our eye. So, how do we accurately describe something we can't see, touch, taste, smell, or hear? Wait, we've been down this road before. It appears that love is also a slippery fish.

I think the author of 1 John would wholeheartedly agree. As a matter of fact, in 1 John 4:16 he writes, *"God is love."* There's our definition. Three short words, but enough for our minds to rest on, and wrestle with, for the remainder of our lives. Here's a verse we can actually memorize with minimal effort. We can use these three words as a mental touchstone as we read through the Bible. We can set them next to things God does and says and meditate on what love really is—and how it may differ from what we may originally have thought.

Chances are, not everything in the Bible, or in our lives, will fall into the nice, neat picture of what we feel a God who is love should look like. Once again, the big God, small brain dilemma strikes home. But sometimes, the reason things don't seem to line up is because we have mangled those three little words we thought were so easy to memorize. We've contorted *"God is love"* into "love is god."

When love becomes our god, we feel the best way to love others is to make them happy. That is, we choose the nice thing over the right thing—and we expect God to do the same. We want the Author of life to write Himself into our story as the ultimate romantic, fashioning life here on earth into a never-ending honeymoon. We reason that if God really loved us, He would prevent anything from happening that would break our hearts. After all, if He has the power to keep us safe and happy, why wouldn't He want to use that power for those He loves?

When my daughter, Katrina, first went away to college, she hit some really low times. Bottom-of-the-barrel low. As a mom who loves her kids deeply, my initial, impulsive thought was to snatch my daughter back from college, lock her in the basement, and feed her a steady supply of snack cakes for the rest of her life—to keep her safe and happy. Obviously, my irrational plan would do neither. What felt like a "nice" thing was a far cry from the right thing.

Instead, I prayed and Katrina stayed. Over time, I saw her mature in wonderful new ways. That didn't mean the hard times were over. Along that bumpy road to growth, my daughter's heart would ache and break. And since I love her, my own heart ached and broke right along with hers. I don't know why brokenness is so often the path to growth. What I do know is that God, in His wisdom that towers so immeasurably above my own, somehow seems to have set it up that way.

Now, whenever I happen upon a box of her favorite snack cakes on a grocery store shelf, I think about that season of Katrina's life and about how true love, God's love, chooses right over nice. (And I also ponder the fact that Katrina doesn't care all that much for those cakes. I'm the one who snarfed them by the truckload as a kid. I haven't eaten one in over a decade, but I suddenly have an insatiable urge to head to the nearest store. I bet a neuropsychologist could really have a heyday with this.)

Although it's a bit embarrassing to admit, those snack cakes have wound up as an unexpected, and unconventional, touchstone for me. They help set my mind on choosing to do what is loving by choosing to do what is right. In our fishing net verse of Philippians 4:8, the Greek word that is translated "right" is *díkaios* which describes whatever is just, honest, and right between people, and in society as a whole. A *díkaios* kind of righteous action is taken not because of the threat of punishment or a wish to keep the peace or be nice, but because of choices an individual imposes upon him- or herself to conform to the will and nature of God.

Díkaios is faith in action, revealing itself through our love for others.

Love God and love others. Got it. We can't forget that. It's so simple, especially with snack cakes to remind us. Right?

Amazing Gracie

If Snow White were looking for an understudy to play her dwarf buddy Grumpy, this particular morning I could have won the part before even rising out of bed. Unfortunately, by the time I'd eaten breakfast, I also seemed to be channeling Grumpy's lesser-known twin, Whiney. Out of obedience (but devoid of expectation), I did spend time in prayer and reading the Bible, but neither seemed to stir an ounce of awe. I flat out told God that all I really wanted to do was go for a drive and listen to loud music. I was in a bad mood and I was determined not to budge from that spot. Then the phone rang.

It was my father. At the sound of his voice, I instantly added a third dwarf to the two who had appeared in my living room that morning: Suspicious. My father usually called when he needed a favor. This morning was no exception. My dad (who lived in another state) wanted me to drive about a half hour away to pick up a specialized part he needed for something or other having to do with his business. And, by the way, I'd need to write a check for a couple of hundred dollars to pay for the part and then go to the post office and overnight the package back to him in California. And, oh yes, he'd reimburse me. Sometime.

By the time I hung up the phone, my emotions were mimicking an entire ensemble cast of dysfunctional dwarves: Grumpy, Whiney, Suspicious, Ticked, and Mumbling. I brusquely grabbed my car keys off the counter and hopped into my hand-me-down Ford Bronco, with the windows that wouldn't roll down, the automatic door locks I had to force down by hand, and the nonfunctioning air-conditioning. Did I mention that the car also had a habit of unexpectedly turning off on its own, usually in the middle of rush-hour traffic?

But one thing that did work was the radio. So there I was, out for a drive and listening to music—loud. That's when it hit me. I was doing exactly what I'd talked to God about this morning. Overwhelmed with a sense of gratitude, remorse, and God's sense of humor, God and I had a do-over quiet time. And it was good.

God helped me be honest enough with myself to see that if a friend had called that morning with the same request as my father, I would have dropped everything and stepped up to help in a nanosecond. And chances are that even if I happened to be in a bad mood, I wouldn't have resented a friend asking me for help. It dawned on me that I needed to willingly extend the same grace and love to my own father that I would to my friends.

I had an authentic smile on my face by the time I walked into the car dealership to pick up the mystery part. But the real clincher to the morning was that the part I went to pick up for my father turned out to be a set of car keys—to a brand-new, bright yellow, black pin-striped, turbocharged VW Bug, complete with a bud vase and killer stereo system. Best of all, it came with a paid-in-full pink slip with my name on it.

Can there be any question as to why I named my Bug Gracie? Six years later, she remains a significant touchstone in my life. When I get behind the wheel and turn on that stereo system, I'm reminded to extend grace and love not only to my father, but to anyone I'm tempted to turn my back on—to offer to others what God has so freely offered to me.

Looking back, I had several choices when my father called. I could have flat out said no to his request. I could have immediately responded with a loving servant's spirit and a wholehearted yes. Or I could have done what I originally did—said yes with my mouth while at the same time shouted a silent no with my heart. (Brings to mind certain verses from the Sermon on the Mount, does it not?) Knowing the right, loving thing to do and doing it are two totally separate things. But when both our mind and our actions line up with God's will, that's when true obedience—and love—take place.

The Fight for What's Right

Getting my mind in line with what's right is an ongoing struggle. It's as though I can hear the author of Hebrews speaking directly to me:

> "You don't seem to listen, so it's hard to make you understand. You have been Christians a long time now, and you ought to be teaching others. Instead, you need someone to teach you again the basic things a beginner must learn about the Scriptures. You are like babies who drink only milk and cannot eat solid food. And a person who is living on milk isn't very far along in the Christian life and doesn't know much about doing what is right. Solid food is for those who are mature, who have trained themselves to recognize the difference between right and wrong and then do what is right."
> —Hebrews 5:11–14 (NLT)

It takes training—mental training—to recognize the difference between what's right and wrong (between what's loving and simply nice) and then to do the right thing. Even the secular philosopher Plato recognized this relationship. He taught that sobriety (which is a sound, mentally fit mind) was directly linked with one's ability to live a righteous (*dikaios*) life.

For me, Plato's emphasis on being mentally sober

automatically paints in my mind a picture of its polar opposite—a mind that's intoxicated with overindulgence. Here, every thought and whim is pampered and coddled. Right and wrong are relative. "If it feels good, do it" is the only rule worth following. To me, this kind of aimless, unsettled, live-for-the-moment kind of thinking seems to be a symptom of someone who is "drunk" on the world.

In contrast, 2 Corinthians 10:5 gives us a picture of how a sober, trained mind responds: *"We demolish arguments and every pretension that sets itself up against the knowledge of God, and we take captive every thought to make it obedient to Christ."*

Anytime we talk about taking something captive, one thing is certain; there's a battle going on. But we're not fighting this battle alone or without the appropriate weaponry. *"For though we live in the world, we do not wage war as the world does. The weapons we fight with are not weapons of the world. On the contrary, they have divine power to demolish strongholds"* (2 Corinthians 10:3–4).

A *stronghold* is just another word for a fortress. And like a physical fortress that is protected by armed warriors and built in a secure, defensible spot, like the top of a hill, we build mental strongholds. Each one is a fortress constructed of falsehood. Some lies may sit relatively unnoticed, and unchallenged, for years. But start taking every thought captive to make it obedient to Christ and an all-out war is declared.

Ephesians 6:12 reminds us that *"our struggle is not against flesh and blood, but against the rulers, against the authorities, against the powers of this dark world and against the spiritual forces of evil in the heavenly realms."* But there's no cause for alarm. Remember, the weapons we're entrusted with have divine power to demolish strongholds. That doesn't mean we can sit back and grab a bowl of popcorn. We're told to "put on" God's armor. We are part of this battle, not mere onlookers.

Taking a closer look at the spiritual weapons we have at our disposal, as described in Ephesians 6:10–18, is something

I encourage you to do on your own, preferably with a Bible commentary close at hand. But right now, there's one offensive weapon we need to take special note of. In Ephesians 6:14, Paul calls one part of the armor God provides us by the term *"breastplate of righteousness."* In a suit of armor, the breastplate is often made up of two pieces, one covering the front and the other the back. The breastplate covers all of a warrior's vital organs, from the neck all the way down to the thighs. Most importantly, the breastplate protects the heart.

Our scriptural "heart" is really in our head. Neurologists refer to it as the limbic system. It is the emotional part of our brains, the seat of our passions, our pleasures, and our pain. It's also the part where thought becomes action. Our heart can push us to place nice over right. Somehow, righteousness helps keep these passions safe and in check, allowing us to "stand firm" during spiritual battle. Though theologians debate whether our breastplate is made up of Christ's righteousness, our own *dikaios* action, or a combination of the two, there's one thing everyone can agree on: Right matters. A lot.

So, why would we hesitate any longer? Let's don our metaphorical armor and boldly take every thought captive to Christ! But what does that really mean? How do we train ourselves to recognize right from wrong? How do we realistically fight a war where the primary battleground lies between our ears?

THE BATTLEGROUND OF OUR BRAINS

If we were faced with a physical battle, one of the first things we'd do is come up with a battle plan. To fight a spiritual battle our strategy is the same. We consider what is at stake and how best to defend it or rescue it. In this case, we develop a strategy to help train ourselves to recognize right and nice. Then, we monitor our progress over time, evaluating our plan's effectiveness by taking a critical look at how what we are setting our mind on is actually playing out in our lives.

This is going to take more than the occasional snack cake.

Honestly, I know of no touchstone more powerful to help me consistently set my mind on whatever is right than memorizing Scripture. That's not to say that I can rattle off the Pentateuch at the drop of a yarmulke or always remember the reference for a verse that pops into my head when a controversial situation arises. But the good news is that verses of Scripture have started popping into my head when I need them most.

My personal strategy begins with reading the Bible over and over, cover to cover, in a variety of translations. I read more than just the portions that tickle my literary fancy or the verses that fit my own personal philosophy. I read books like Leviticus, Numbers, Deuteronomy, and Revelation. I spend time with sections of Scripture that leave me scratching my head and feeling like a theological toddler. I may not "get" it all, but I have read it all.

As I mentioned in the last chapter, this isn't something I do every spare moment of the day. I simply read a few chapters every morning. I take time to think and pray about what I've read and contemplate how God's ways differ from my own. I consider how I need to realign my view of right—and how I can act on what I've heard. God admonishes us:

> *"Do not merely listen to the word, and so deceive yourselves. Do what it says. Anyone who listens to the word but does not do what it says is like a man who looks at his face in a mirror and, after looking at himself, goes away and immediately forgets what he looks like. But the man who looks intently into the perfect law that gives freedom, and continues to do this, not forgetting what he has heard, but doing it—he will be blessed in what he does."*
> —James 1:22–25

One of the principal issues people fight for is freedom. James reminds us that in the spiritual battle we're engaged in, God's perfect law is a key to freedom. *"[Looking] intently into the perfect law"* means looking intently at the Bible. Continuing to do this (repetition) and figuring out how we can apply this to our lives (relevance) will help us remember what is right. As an added bonus, we'll be blessed in what we do!

In the last year or so, I've altered my Bible reading plan a bit to help embed God's words more permanently in my mind. When I read a verse that I want to come more alive in my life, I write it onto a 3-by-5 card. Then, I put these cards into one of those inexpensive little photo albums. Though I'm still working on becoming more consistent in this area, my goal is to try to spend time each day reading these verses aloud.

If you ask my friends, they'll tell you that I'm not known for my structured and methodical approach to life. I'm more of a free-spirit kind of gal. But even a free spirit has to get herself organized and in shape when she's faced with war. And there's a battle going on. I can feel it when I struggle with knowing the right thing to do and choosing the right way to love.

I don't want my gray matter filled with gray areas. I want to do the right thing when it comes to loving God and others. Though Gracie and snack cakes may temporarily help refocus my thoughts in a skirmish, only God's Word is going to help me win the war. For only God and His Word have the power to set this free spirit free.

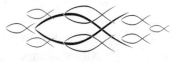

Deep "C" Fishing

This chapter is far from the last word on right and wrong. It's only an appetizer, something to whet your appetite for righteousness. To get your mental juices flowing in that direction, it's important to act on what you've heard. Time to don your armor, come up with a battle plan, and then fight for what's right.

1. Let your mind rest for awhile on this:

   Preparing your minds for action, and being sober-minded, set your hope fully on the grace that will be brought to you at the revelation of Jesus Christ. As obedient children, do not be conformed to the passions of your former ignorance, but as he who called you is holy, you also be holy in all your conduct.
   —1 Peter 1:13–15 (ESV)

   - In Greek, *"preparing your minds for action"* more literally means "girding up the loins of your mind." In our modern-day lingo, this sounds rather comical. But what does this phrase actually mean? What kind of mental picture does "girding up the loins of your mind" paint for you? What is one concrete action you can take to do this?

- In Ephesians 6:10–18, we're told four times to "stand." How does being sober-minded help us stand our ground?

- Is there any particular issue you're battling at the moment in which you're having trouble deciding the right thing to do? Using a topical concordance (often found at the back of your Bible), write down at least three verses that apply to your struggle. Spend time this week repeating, meditating on, and praying over these verses. Not every area of life slides easily into a clear-cut, black or white, right or wrong box. That's one reason why becoming more consistent in setting our minds on whatever is right is so crucial. The better we get to know God's Word, and His heart, the better we'll be able to discern which way to turn when we're facing complex life issues.

2. The Greek word *díkaios* refers not only to doing the right thing in relationships but also doing right things as a member of society. Read 1 Peter 2:13–17 and Mark 12:13–17. What do these verses have to say about social responsibility?

- Do these verses bring to mind any areas you need to make right in your life?

- What do these verses imply about being environmentally responsible? Following traffic laws? Downloading music? Paying your taxes? Voting?

- Romans 14:23 in *The Message* says, *"If the way you live isn't consistent with what you believe, then it's wrong."* What does God have to say to you personally through this verse?

3. As we focus on whatever is right, we need to be cautious not to slide from the mind-set of grace into legalism. We are under the New Covenant, not the Old. Read Ephesians 2:8–9 aloud: *"It is by grace you have been saved, through faith—and this not of yourselves, it is the gift of God—not by works, so that no one can boast."*

- What does legalism mean to you? What do you think it means to God?

- How can legalism lead to judging others? What does God have to say about anyone in the judgment seat other than Himself? (Support your answer with at least two verses of Scripture.) Why do you think God speaks so strongly about this?

- Choose your weapon—one of the verses you've read today. Embed this scriptural touchstone deeply into your mind by memorizing God's words in the way that works best for you. Don't just toy with your weapon—learn to wield it skillfully. Meditate on it. Talk about it with your friends and family. Journal about what God teaches you through it. Use it to guard your heart.

CHAPTER SEVEN

FROM ASHES TO AWESTRUCK

"Whatever is pure."
—Philippians 4:8

It looks like Little Foot is going to have babies," my husband explained to our young son. "She's going to be a mommy!" Ryan spontaneously burst into tears. Not quite the response Mark and I were expecting when we'd decided to tell our son why his pet guinea pig was packing on the pounds.

"Why are you upset?" I asked.

Ryan wiped his eyes with his tiny, balled fists and replied, "Because I missed Little Foot's wedding at the pet store!" Ah, the innocence of childhood...

In our minds, innocence and purity are as inextricably bound together as motherhood and marriage were for Ryan at age six. But as adults, our own childhood innocence is a thing of the past. To set our minds on *"whatever is pure,"* we need to be as intentional as we were when we chose to set our minds on whatever is right.

Purity and righteousness are actually two sides of the same spiritual coin. While *díkaios* refers to the right thing between members of society, *hagnós* (the Greek word we translate as "pure" in Philippians 4:8), means to be innocent, chaste, and blameless in both thought and action, particularly as it relates to the opposite sex. *Hagnós* is also closely related to the word *hágios*, which means holy and flawless.

Whether blameless or flawless, innocent or holy, when I set my mind on whatever is pure my initial reaction is more of a question: Who, me?

HOW SEXY AM I?

How could I not look? Each foot was the size of my VW Bug. As I drove down the freeway, the billboard with two pair of feet, one set male and the other female, all sprawled out from beneath rumpled bed sheets, caught my attention. But it was the caption that sent my mind into overdrive: "How sexy am I?"

What was this billboard advertising? An online dating service? It looked more like an escort service, perhaps one with a dot-com address or 900 number. Was it a link to a plastic surgeon? A counseling office? Free medication for erectile dysfunction? One thing was certain. I wasn't about to log on. It was almost as hard keeping unwanted junk off my computer's hard drive as it was out of my thoughts.

A few weeks later I learned this provocative billboard was sponsored by a local church. Obviously, it piqued other motorists' curiosity as easily as it did mine. Over 2,000 people not only logged onto the Web site, but also visited the church's weekend services to learn more about God's design for sex. Smart marketing. The motto Sex Sells isn't just hype.

But in a society where sex is used to sell everything from cars to deodorant to a sermon series, is purity still relevant? Or is it simply relative? Does whatever is pure ebb and flow with the changing tides of social norms? In God's eyes, how sexy are we?

If we read the Bible, there seems to be no doubt that as members of the human race, you and I are sexy people. God designed us that way; then He said, "*It is very good.*"

Yes, sex is good. But without purity, it gets twisted into something less than it was designed to be. Purity, like righteousness, has to do with right relationship. Throughout both the Old and New Testaments, the "right" relationship for sexual intimacy is described as marriage. But throughout Scripture, lots of people, even godly people, strayed from this original design. Sarah encouraged Abraham to have sex with her servant, Hagar, to conceive a surrogate son. Lot offered his two virgin daughters to a lustful mob of men to try to dissuade them from having sex with the family's male visitors. Later, Lot's daughters got their father drunk and became pregnant by him. David had an affair with Bathsheba. David's son Amnon, raped his half sister, Tamar. Solomon, another one of David's sons, had 700 wives and 300 concubines. And it doesn't end there.

Though the New Testament doesn't name names as frequently as the Old Testament, there are enough references to sexual impurity to let us know that having God's law written on our hearts and minds didn't put an end to this problem. Far from it. If we have any doubt, all we need to do is take a look at Paul's letters to the church at Corinth.

In the first century, Corinth was the Las Vegas of the ancient world. It had a reputation as a haven for uninhibited self-indulgence, especially in relation to sex. There was even a slang Greek term for sexual immorality that meant "to act like a Corinthian." Obviously, the concept of biblical purity would be considered outside the norm in this kind of culture. Fast-forward 2,000 years.

Today, living together is not only regarded as generally acceptable, but prudent, especially if you're considering marriage. And if you don't happen to be in a serious relationship, you have the option of "hooking up" or having "friends with benefits" to help quell those sexual urges. After all, sex is simply a physical need, like hunger and thirst. Like other animals, we're merely responding to our instinct for preservation.

Obviously, I'm playing the devil's advocate here. I believe God wove sexual intimacy and relationship together in a beautiful and mysterious way. And how can we "become one" with someone physically without being affected mentally and emotionally?

First Corinthians 6:16–20 from *The Message* sums this up better than I ever could:

> *"There's more to sex than mere skin on skin. Sex is as much a spiritual mystery as a physical fact. As written in Scripture, 'The two become one.' Since we want to become spiritually one with the Master, we must not pursue the kind of sex that avoids commitment and intimacy, leaving us more lonely than ever—the kind of sex that can never 'become one.' There is a sense in which sexual sins are different from all others. In sexual sin we violate the sacredness of our own bodies, these bodies that were made for God-given and God-modeled love, for 'becoming one' with another. Or didn't you realize that your body is a sacred place, the place of the Holy Spirit? Don't you see that you can't live however you please, squandering what God paid such a high price for? The physical part of you is not some piece of property belonging to the spiritual part of you. God owns the whole works. So let people see God in and through your body."*
> —1 Corinthians 6:16–20

In the original Greek, Paul uses the word *naos* in verse 19 when he talks about our bodies being a *"sacred place, the place of the Holy Spirit."* This is the same word used in Scripture for the holy of holies in the Jewish temple,

The holy of holies was the purest and most sacred room in the whole temple. It was the place where God's presence dwelled. The thought of sex sanctioned to take place in the holy of holies certainly elevates physical intimacy to a higher plane. This is far from animal instinct. This borders on worship.

To set our minds on purity, we do not need to "cleanse" our minds of sex. We simply need to train ourselves to default to God's perspective, instead of the Corinthians'. For me, the mental image of my body as the holy of holies is a strong one. It was this image, aided by the touchstone of a thin, silver band on my ring finger that helped me remain steadfast in my choice to refrain from premarital sex. It's true that 30 years ago, social mores were quite a bit more straitlaced. But some people still thought Mark and I were nuts—including my parents.

Even before I met Mark, my parents encouraged me to take birth-control pills when I went away to college "so nothing would happen." When I tried to convince them that "nothing would happen," because I wasn't going to let anything else happen beforehand, they looked at me like I had Jell-O for brains. When they encouraged Mark and me to live together before we got married and we chose not to, they emphatically rolled their eyes.

Then, Mark and I broke off our engagement. It wasn't because we decided not to get married, but because we felt as though our relationship was moving too fast. (Granted, on our first date we not only talked about marriage, but also picked out the name Ryan for our potential future son!) We decided to wait one year before discussing marriage again.

However, taking off my engagement ring didn't disconnect my mind, my emotions, and my physical attraction from Mark. So I bought a ring to wear in its place, one that would serve as a tangible reminder to me of whom I was truly committed to. For the next year I wore a silver band, engraved with *Jesus* on my ring finger. I vowed to wear that ring until I felt certain God would approve of my replacing it with a wedding band. A year later, I believe He did.

Seventeen years later, my daughter, Katrina, turned 12. At that time, I spoke frankly with her about sex, purity, and true love—and gave her the silver ring I'd worn during the year Mark and I were "disengaged." I'll never forget her response.

"Don't worry about me," she said. "Remember, the name Katrina means 'pure one.'"

Today, even though Katrina is married, she continues to wear the silver ring, which she hopes to pass on to her own daughter some day. This ring is not a secret weapon to self-control. It's simply a touchstone, a reminder to think before we act, to be physically pure in our relationships with the opposite sex.

I believe the choices my daughter and I made before marriage continue to have positive repercussions in our marriages today. I believe there are some battles we will not have to fight and some temptations that will hold less allure for us. But that doesn't mean all's quiet on the sexual battlefront. It also doesn't mean I'm more pure in God's eyes than those who may have lost this particular battle. Whatever is pure goes so much deeper than that.

99 Percent Pure

For years, whenever I heard the word *pure* I pictured a bar of soap. Apparently, all those commercials featuring a snow white, sudsy bath bar that was "99 percent pure—so pure it floats!" really made an impression on me as a kid. I wasn't the only one. Marketing Ivory soap based on its purity began way back in 1881 as the brainchild of Harley Procter. As the son of Procter & Gamble's cofounder, Harley obviously knew the power of a good scientific testimonial to help sell cleaning products.

However, there were no standards on what pure soap was. So, Harley hired a scientific consultant to set a standard. The consultant decided that pure soap would consist only of fatty acids and alkali, the most common ingredients used in manufacturing soap at that time. Using this as the scientific criteria, Ivory soap did prove to be more pure than some of the popular castile soaps of the day, which often included natural oils. The firm declared Ivory "99 and $^{44}/_{100}$ percent pure" and a marketing slogan was born. (And, in case you're interested,

Ivory floats because it has air mixed into it. Its buoyancy has nothing to do with purity.)

But can something really be 99 and $^{44}/_{100}$ percent pure? By definition, the word *pure* implies total freedom from defilements and impurities. Either something is pure or it's not. Like Ivory soap, you and I are not 100 percent pure, no matter how many chaste choices, loving actions, or godly thoughts we've packed into our lifetimes. As 1 John 1:8 (NLT) so clearly states, *"If we say we have no sin, we are only fooling ourselves and refusing to accept the truth."*

The Greek word for *sin* literally means "to miss the mark." Like an arrow that overshoots a bull's-eye and winds up in the weeds, I miss God's perfect mark for my life on a daily basis. Even on those days when my life looks pretty good on the outside, I know what takes place on the inside—and it isn't even 99 and $^{44}/_{100}$ percent pure.

However, the reality of 1 John 1:8 is followed by the promise of verse 9 (NLT): *"But if we confess our sins to him, he is faithful and just to forgive us and to cleanse us from every wrong."* If you've dared to venture this far into this book, chances are you probably have a pretty clear idea as to how this cleansing takes place. As 1 Peter 3:18 assures us, *"Christ died for sins once for all, the righteous for the unrighteous, to bring you to God."* Unlike the high priests who brought sacrificial offerings to God again and again to cleanse the people of Israel from their sins, Christ cleansed us for all eternity through His death on the Cross.

So, we confess. We're cleansed by Christ's sacrifice. God forgives us, once and for all. Then, we're home free—100 percent purified and 100 percent forgiven in God's eyes.

But, when it comes to the word *confess* there's something that often gets lost in translation. In 1 John 1:9, *confess* is a present active subjunctive. Now, if you're like me, a grammatical sentence diagram dropout, this means absolutely nothing. However, that doesn't mean it isn't important. In this verse, the word *confess* is not a one-time action. It's like the

Energizer bunny. It's something that keeps going and going and going. That doesn't mean I need to confess the same sin over and over again, but I do need to keep coming to God in confession on a regular basis.

But if God's already forgiven us and He knows our every thought, word, and deed, why should we keep confessing? After all, what's done is done, both the sin and the forgiveness.

I believe confession is a God-given touchstone. It's like a compass I check now and again to make sure I'm still headed in the right direction. It doesn't require a confessional, a priest, or an appointment. All I need to do is set my pride aside so I can come honestly and humbly before God's throne, and then agree with what God has to say about how I've missed the mark He's set for my life.

Talking to God about where I've blown it does three things. It helps me realign my perspective with God's. It removes any false guilt I've been lugging around by reminding me that I'm forgiven. And it helps lead me toward repentance. To *repent* means to "turn around." God's compass of confession is a gift that sets me straight by literally turning my life around.

I still vividly recall a time of confession I shared with God almost a decade ago. Being a rather visual person, and since God is such an invisible Sovereign, as I talked to God about how I'd missed His mark in my life, a picture began to develop in my mind's eye. I was standing before Jesus, relaying to Him all of the guilt and shame I'd been lugging around for way too long. Some of it was unjustified. Much of it was well earned. I wanted to hand all of these transgressions, big and small, real and imagined, over to Jesus. I didn't want to carry them any longer. I didn't need to carry them at all.

When I looked at my hands, raised as if to present Jesus with an offering of repentance, I saw that they were filled with ashes. My heart broke as I came to the deep realization of how unworthy the offering I was presenting was to One so perfectly holy. Ashamed, I slowly raised my eyes from the ashes and looked into Jesus's face. What I saw was unabashed love and acceptance.

As I placed the ashes into Jesus's outstretched hands, His face broke into a wide smile. He raised His ash-filled hands to the sky—and the ashes transformed into a snow-white dove that disappeared into the clouds. To this day I remember how pure, free, and loved I felt at that moment.

I know that some people may classify my confession experience as simply the product of an overactive imagination. Others may even feel it wholly inappropriate to use any type of visualization when we pray. All I know is that with sincerity of heart I laid my sins before God and I believe He gave me a touchstone in return. For me, the sight of ashes now serves as a reminder of everything God has so graciously forgiven me.

Let me assure you that not every time I confess winds up as a Technicolor mental movie. Most of the time it's comprised solely of a heartfelt apology. And, unfortunately, there are times I bypass confession altogether. Instead, I head straight to self-justification.

I've Got a Secret

Self-justification is sneaky. It lurks in dim, hidden corners, but when exposed to the light has been known to strut around as proudly as a supermodel who's recently mastered the art of stilettos. It masquerades as righteousness, when it's anything but. It's pride cloaked in faux humility, deceit proclaiming it's an angel of light. And if it garners a following, beware. It's known to be highly contagious.

Self-justification is an enemy of purity. It can be like a Black Op (yes, I watch *NCIS*), under deep cover and camouflaged to the point of being almost invisible to the untrained eye—or mind. That's why training our brains to recognize whatever is pure is so important. It's along the same lines as what those NCIS agents do to help them better recognize counterfeit bills—they study the real thing. The more easily we recognize genuine purity, the more we'll see self-justification for what it truly is: an arrow in the weeds impersonating a bull's-eye.

The English language provides its own tiny touchstone to help us spot our kind of justification. It's a word within a word, the word *just*. The more we set our sights on purity, the more our ears will perk up when we hear: "It's *just* a kiss." "*Just* try it, no one will know." "It's not like I'm addicted to porn; I'm *just* appreciating the beauty of the opposite sex." "It's *just* a little skin."

There was a time in my life (a few months before my ashes-to-dove confession), when I tried justifying my own actions with the words, "They're *just* scratches. It's not like I'm cutting myself with scissors or anything like that." I was a young mother, struggling with panic attacks, nightmares, and impure memories that seemed to wrap me in a heavy cloak of shame. When the ache inside seemed too heavy to bear, I'd scratch long lines with my fingernails along my inner arms. For a moment, the burn of broken skin on the outside took my mind off the gnawing ache inside.

Since it was winter, long sleeves hid my self-destructive pastime. But one day, my self-hatred reached a new low. Almost instinctively, I dragged my long fingernails down the sides of my face. I panicked as I ran to the mirror. Long red streaks reached from the corner of my eyes down to my jaw line. People would see. People would know. The shame I'd felt earlier intensified.

But my fears were unfounded. No one noticed. I had long hair, so I simply lowered my head when I was around other people. I found a way to hide in broad daylight—and that scared me. At that point, I recognized I'd come to a crossroads. I could move toward God or away from Him. There was no other option. Confess or justify myself. I chose to confess.

After God and I had a long chat, I decided to take my confession a step further. I told the counselor I was seeing at the time what I'd done, and what I had been doing for months. Once I admitted my secret aloud, something truly amazing happened. That secret lost its hold over me.

If I was living in Old Testament times, chances are at this point I would have built an altar or stacked a pile of stones to commemorate this turning point God had brought me to. Instead, I chose a different kind of visual touchstone. I cut my hair. It was kind of a reverse Nazirite move. Nazirites were Jews who made a vow before God that included *not* cutting their hair. This was a symbolic way of setting themselves apart for the Lord, a visual touchstone in their pursuit of purity.

My touchstone wasn't as noticeable as the Nazirites'. I didn't don a Mohawk, shave my head, or do anything radically different. I simply had my hair cut short enough so that it could no longer serve as a hiding place. I wanted to be able to look people, and God, in the eye. I wanted to be diligent in my pursuit of purity and transparent in how I lived my life. But I was, and continue to be, forgetful. (Have I mentioned that before? I forget...) Seeing my short hair in the mirror continues to serve as a daily reminder that I want to be someone void of secrets.

Like the word *just*, secrets can serve as a touchstone to change. Anytime we become aware of something in our lives—or even our thoughts—that we'd prefer to keep hidden from those around us, chances are we've uncovered a stronghold of impurity. At this point we have a choice—conceal or confess, rationalize or repent.

Bringing my secret out into the open didn't instantly solve all my problems. I still had days when I ached inside and, on occasion, felt the familiar pull to hurt myself. But, after I brought what I'd hidden into the light, any type of self-justification rang so hollow that it was easy to "just say no." Knowing my counselor was there to help keep me accountable helped, as well. Through her, I experienced the power of James 5:16 (*The Message*): *"Confess your sins to each other and pray for each other so that you can live together whole and healed."*

Confessing our sins to one another is not something to be taken lightly. The things we do in secret can be dark and destructive. Sharing them with someone else can be like handing that person a time bomb. Those who are not mature enough to know how to defuse this information properly, with the help of Scripture and God's Spirit of wisdom, can actually suffer from the fallout. It can lead their minds, and sometimes even their actions, away from whatever is pure.

This doesn't mean that only a professional counselor is qualified to take on the role of accountability partner, though in certain circumstances this may be extremely helpful. A spouse, close friend, or mentor may be the spiritual sounding board we need to help us make the U-turn of true repentance and get back on the road to what is right and pure.

Sharing our secret struggles takes communication to a very intimate level. That's why it's best to reserve this level of conversation for confidants of the same sex, unless the other person happens to be our spouse or a professional counselor. Remember, God created us as sexy people. I've known way too many godly men and women who've started off as *just* friends, but their intimate conversations led them down relational rabbit holes they never intended to explore. Some of these relationships became physical. Others did not. I won't play a Sermon-on-the-Mount-inspired judge as to whether the latter lusted in their hearts. All I know is that more often than not, hearts were broken and purity was put on the line.

If we're sincere about setting our minds on whatever is pure, we need to venture beyond mental exercises and building neural connections. We need to become more proactive in our choices about where we go, what we do, and who we're intimate with, whether physically or verbally. We need to act on the words of 2 Timothy 2:22 (NLT): *"Run from anything that stimulates youthful lusts. Instead, pursue righteous living, faithfulness, love, and peace. Enjoy the companionship of those who call on the Lord with pure hearts."*

SINGLE-MINDED SIGHT

I'd been crying all week and it was starting to get on my nerves. So I brought it up to my counselor. I casually mentioned that

I wanted to be more aware of God's presence, to see His fingerprints more readily in my day-to-day life. So, I'd been praying very consistently that God would purify my heart. After all, in the Sermon on the Mount, Jesus said the *"pure in heart"* would not only be blessed, but they'd see God.

My dear, wise counselor shook her head at me. It was something I was used to by now. Then, she asked softly, "What did you think purifying your heart would be like?"

Honestly, I'd never really given it much thought. I answered her question with a question: "A bubble bath...?"

OK, so I was a little naïve. Being pure in heart sounds so soft and innocent, snow-white and gentle, kind of like a bubbly bar of floating soap. In reality, the act of purification more often involves fire and ashes, boiling and melting, vigorously straining impurities that rise to the surface. When it comes to purifying gold, this process is repeated until the goldsmith can see a reflection of his own face in the molten metal.

Asking God to help make us pure in heart is not a prayer to be taken lightly. But it's a prayer I continue to pray. I want God to see His image reflected more clearly in me. Although I'm wholly pure in His eyes when it comes to matters of salvation, impurities continue to rise to the surface in my life. And I continue to make the choice as to whether I will remove what God reveals or let it sink back beneath the surface, only to rise again another day.

In Scripture, the term *pure in heart* actually has at least a double meaning. As we already know, it means to be chaste in our thoughts and actions. But the phrase is also used to describe someone who is single-minded and free from deceit. If I am single-minded in my commitment to God and to who He created me to be, righteousness and purity will become inevitable hallmarks of my life.

As I mentioned before, whatever is right and whatever is pure are really flip sides of the same coin—and justification is the plug nickel. The more we view our bodies, which includes our minds, as God's holy of holies, the stronger desire we'll have to keep that temple clean and pure. No dark corners. No secret stash. No hypocrisy.

Titus 1:15–16 (NLT) says,
> *"Everything is pure to those whose hearts are pure. But nothing is pure to those who are corrupt and unbelieving, because their minds and their consciences are defiled. Such people claim they know God, but they deny him by the way they live. They are detestable and disobedient, worthless for doing anything good."*

The same verse in *The Message* describes those who are impure this way:
> *"They leave dirty fingerprints on every thought and act. They say they know God, but their actions speak louder than their words."*
> —Titus 1:15–16 (*The Message*)

Ouch.

There's a T-shirt motto that reads, "Did you ever stop to consider that the purpose of your life might be to serve as a warning to others?" I don't want to be the fool from Proverbs, whose life serves as a cautionary tale. I don't want a mind and conscience that's defiled. I want to be a living touchstone that points the way toward heaven, one on whom God bestows a crown of beauty instead of ashes. I want to single-mindedly pursue purity, so I can catch a glimpse of the invisible God, and others can better see God's image reflected in me.

Deep "C" Fishing

Exploring whatever is pure can be quite a workout for our minds, our hearts, our relationships, and our lifestyles. Like righteousness, purity is not a relaxing vacation spot we let our minds drift off to every once in awhile to help us draw closer to God. Purity is more like a lifelong marathon that we need to mentally train ourselves to run each and every day. So, take a deep breath and continue putting one metaphorical foot in front of the other.

1. Spend some time thinking and praying about your body as a sacred place, God's temple, the holy of holies, as described in 1 Corinthians 6:19–20.

• Paul continues this message in 2 Corinthians 6:16 when he writes, *"We are the temple of the living God."* How does picturing yourself this way change how you view your body? Your mind? Other people?

• How might this image change how you dress? Eat? Exercise? Attend to your health?

- Though how we use, or abuse, our bodies is important, how can external piety in this area become a counterfeit for internal purity?

2. When we choose to set our minds on whatever is pure, we can easily slide into the same legalistic, judgmental mind-set that we saw as a potential problem when setting our minds on whatever is right. Before you read the Scripture below, prepare your mind by asking God to help you be open to what He personally wants you to learn.

- Read Luke 6:37–42. What does this section of Scripture have to say about becoming God's "purity police" in the lives of others? Which verse strikes home most closely with you? Why?

- Some people are very vocal about certain sexual practices being an abomination in God's eyes, using the word to imply that some sins are greater than others. What verses of Scripture can you find to refute or support this point of view?

- In the Bible, the word *abomination* is interchangeable with the word *detestable*. Consider Proverbs 16:5 (ESV), which states, *"Everyone who is arrogant . . . is an abomination to the Lord."* How are arrogance and judging others related?

3. We've spent a good part of this chapter focusing on how to spot impurity and what to do when we find it. Now, let's take some time to simply set our minds on whatever is pure.

- Take a few moments to think about the words *pure* and *purity*. What images come to mind?

- Read Psalm 51, the song that beseeches God, *"Create in me a clean heart* (v. 10). David wrote it after he had an affair with Bathsheba. What word pictures does he paint? Writing a song was a touchstone for David that became a touchstone for us. What do you think David wanted to remember? What do you want to remember from the lesson David learned?

- Spend some time with God in both adoration and confession. Consider one tangible touchstone you can implement into your life that will help draw your mind back to whatever is pure.

CHAPTER EIGHT

EVERY MASTERPIECE
NEEDS A MASTER

"Whatever is lovely."
—Philippians 4:8

I have a confession to make. I have not given the word *lovely* its due. I've treated it as a rather wimpy adjective, a *beautiful* wannabe, just a baby step above *nice*. Polite. Dated. Reserved. No depth. No fire. A kindness often used to mask an unpleasant truth. "That's a *lovely* color on you!" (Translation: Although the cut of that dress isn't doing you any favors.) "I had a *lovely* time." (Translation: It was better than sitting around doing nothing on a Saturday night.) "That was a *lovely* meal." (Translation: Guess I'll be stopping by McDonald's on my way home.)

At first glance, *"whatever is lovely"* seemed a bit out of place with the other less tangible, more stoutheartedly significant descriptors listed in Philippians 4:8: Truth. Nobility. Righteousness. Purity. Loveliness? Setting my mind on whatever is lovely evoked images of little girls' tea parties: manners holding giggles in check, the rustle of crinoline frocks, a tower of miniscule cucumber sandwiches, and every girl's pinkie appropriately crooked as she daintily sips Earl Grey from her rosebud-strewn porcelain cup. Whatever is lovely seemed all fluff, no substance.

I was wrong. Loveliness is not the weaker sister of Beautiful. Lovely's power far surpasses that of mere beauty. Lovely may be winsome and aesthetically pleasing, but in its richest sense, *whatever is lovely* describes something that attracts or inspires love. What's more, these "somethings" are often actual things. We can see, hear, touch, taste, and smell what is lovely. At last, we've found ourselves on more solid mental ground! But don't get too excited. Loveliness carries its own set of challenges. Namely, the enticement to shift our focus from loving the Creator to loving what He's created.

TOUCHSTONES IN OIL

Early every spring, artists from all over the country gather in Scottsdale, Arizona. For ten weeks, they use what looks like a giant circus tent as their collective studio. Though the artists exhibit and sell their work in this makeshift gallery, the big draw for the public is the chance to watch, and interact with, the artists as they work in their chosen medium.

One of the artists my husband, Mark, and I enjoy watching each year paints rocks—as in "portrays in oil amazingly realistic-looking stones on canvas." From a distance, and even close-up for that matter, this artist's paintings look like photographs. And every single composition is comprised almost solely of rocks—mostly smooth, river rocks, in tones of gray, black, and white. Not even colorful rocks, distinctive rocks, or rocks you'd be tempted to pick up on a hike and put in your pocket. Simply by studying this artist's work, I can tell that the artist is someone who has caught a glimpse of the extraordinary loveliness God has woven into the seemingly ordinary.

Before I saw this artist's work, I hardly ever gave boring old rocks a second glance. I kicked them now and again. Tried to skim flat ones across ponds when the opportunity arose. Scooped handfuls of them around new plants in the desert-landscaped backyard of our Phoenix home. But classified them as *lovely*? Not a chance.

Once again, I was wrong. And it took a painting to show me the error of my ways. Usually when rocks are in my field of vision, I don't focus on them. I consider them insignificant rubble in the midst of the grand canvas of nature. But this artist confined his "rocks" to a framed canvas. The manageable borders helped me narrow my focus, in turn helping eliminate competing visual and mental distractions. Voilà! For the first time my eyes were opened wide enough, and my mind was focused on something small enough, to really notice the wonder present in common river rocks.

This artist's stones-in-oil became a personal touchstone to something wholly lovely. They helped bring to mind the fact that every common stone is a supernatural work of art that could be used to adorn a riverbed, build the Pyramids of Egypt, or maybe even kill a giant. Rocks (and not even *real* ones) led me to worship the true creative Artist behind each and every stone, the Rock of Ages Himself. These common rocks were not exceptionally beautiful, but they were altogether lovely. They inspired me toward a deeper love of their Creator. And that's what the heart of *lovely* is all about.

The word we translate as "lovely," *prosphilē* in Greek, is found only once in the New Testament—here in Philippians 4:8. *Prosphilē* combines two smaller Greek words: *pros* (meaning a motion toward something) and *philéo* (which describes the love of a deep, enduring friendship.) In the New Testament this word is used to describe the kind of love the disciples had for Jesus. So, setting our minds on whatever is lovely ultimately draws us toward relationship. We'll talk about focusing on whatever is lovely in other people a bit later on. For now, let's continue to practice setting our minds on things above.

GOD'S GALLERY

The universe is God's gallery, crammed full of unparalleled masterpieces. Each unique creation outshines anything found in the galleries of Scottsdale. If an accurate rendering of a simple stone can draw me closer to God, imagine what a glimpse of God's handiwork of the Grand Canyon or a meteor shower can do!

Every work of God's hand is lovely in the truest sense. It's a potential touchstone that can help us focus our minds on God, drawing our hearts closer to His. But for some people, these touchstones can become stumbling blocks. The incomparable beauty of ocean waves beating on a rocky shoreline, a herd of wild mustangs moving as one over a barren plain, or the momentary blaze of a desert sunset can stop us in our tracks. We are rocked by a sense of utter awe. We are being wooed toward God by loveliness. But if we venture no deeper than basking in the beauty of God's creation, we may wind up worshipping at the altar of Mother Nature instead of at our almighty Father's feet.

Romans 1:20 (TNIV) says, *"For since the creation of the world God's invisible qualities—his eternal power and divine nature—have been clearly seen, being understood from what has been made, so that people are without excuse."* God may be a slippery fish. He may be invisible to our human eyes and more immense than our human minds can hold. But He has festooned our visible world with garlands of His glory, tangible evidence of His intangible existence.

Loveliness is God's calling card. It draws us beyond beauty's initial attraction of awe to the inner courtyard of authentic worship. But if we do not consciously engage our minds, setting them on an intentional search for the loveliness that is woven into each of God's creations, we may miss out on the most important part of the journey. Beauty may catch our eye, but it's *lovely* that satisfies; *lovely* draws us toward what's of eternal worth, toward a relationship with God.

One way to set our minds on whatever is lovely is to peruse God's universal gallery like we would a gallery in Scottsdale. When I visit an art gallery or museum, I walk slowly, taking time to note the color and composition of paintings and photography, the cut and curve of sculpture, the texture and symmetry of pottery. I stop, stare, and ponder. I note how old something is, how intricate or delicate it is, how skillfully it's made.

I also find myself making educated guesses about the creators behind the creations. Even without knowing anything about Georgia O'Keeffe, by studying her paintings I can deduce that here is an artist who enjoyed vivid blue skies and stark desert landscapes; a woman who could spend the afternoon appreciating the intricacies of a common flower or listening to the silent message of mortality preached by a sun-bleached cow skull. Though O'Keeffe's paintings are realistic, they are not reality. Flowers are large and loud. Details are suggested rather than painstakingly recreated. My guess is this woman's home would have been filled with "found" treasures, instead of fussy little store-bought knickknacks. I would deduce she liked to live life large, yet with a quiet grace.

To find out if my impressions were accurate, I could read books about Georgia O'Keeffe. I could talk to those who knew her or, if she were still alive, I could talk to her in person. I could also continue to study her body of work, laying the impressions I gathered alongside the information I garnered to see where they were in, and out of, alignment.

I can do the same with God—and so can you. We can study the works of God's hands in light of Romans 1:20. We can ask ourselves, "What does this reveal to me about God's invisible qualities and divine nature?" We can ask those who've walked with God longer than we have, "What is He like?" We can read the Bible to see how these impressions line up with the words of the prophets and the life of Jesus. And we can pray. We can ask the Creator Himself to give us insight into His own character through the lovely touchstones of His creation.

I was originally drawn to Georgia O'Keeffe through the work of her hands. Though I find her art interesting, as time goes on I find the artist behind the artwork much more intriguing. The same is true with God. I was drawn to God's artwork long before I knew Him. But the more I study the touchstones of God's creation, the more intrigued I am by their Creator—and the more I'm drawn to love and worship Him.

Let's take a moment right now for a mental stroll through your own personal wing of God's gallery. Close your eyes and picture the most breathtaking view of nature you've ever beheld. Chat with God about this experience for a few minutes. Express to Him what's lovely about His creation, what specifically draws you to Him. Then, ponder what you can learn about God's character from what you saw, heard, touched, smelled, or even tasted.

Whether I'm taking a mental stroll or a physical one, when I ponder the loveliness of God's creation, one of the first things I'm reminded of is that God has an artist's heart. This implies something important about God's character. It says that He values beauty and creativity. He doesn't consider them a waste of time or space.

My friend Cathy can attest to this in a most unusual way. She's one of those brave and brilliant women who homeschooled her three kids up through high school. One day, for a hands-on project in her children's science unit, Cathy had the unenviable task of dissecting a cow's eye. Cathy tried to convey a sense of excitement and confidence to her kids as she queasily brandished a knife above the apricot-sized eyeball staring back at her from the plastic tub. But once Cathy made the initial incision, her trepidation turned to absolute awe. The inside of this bovine eyeball was filled with an iridescent rainbow of shimmering color that Cathy described as one of the most beautiful things she had ever seen. *Inside* a cow's eye! Not even the cow gets to see it! But that doesn't matter to God—to an Artist who apparently cares deeply about details. Even the inside of an eyeball is lavish with loveliness.

God's extravagance in showering this universe with such a wide variety of beauty (which is only one aspect of loveliness) clearly declares His artistic bent. Consider the northern lights, the Venus flytrap, or the twin-tusked narwhal. God's like a little kid, playfully creating and then sharing what He's made with those He loves.

Yet countless wildflowers bloom in hidden meadows. Unnavigable ocean depths hold whimsical sea creatures humans may never see. Atoms, cells, and galaxies, each a masterpiece of splendor and organization, exist invisible to the naked eye. God creates not only for our pleasure, but for His. That's a true hallmark of an artist's heart.

THE ALMIGHTY ARTIST

God is an artist—and He's also almighty. That makes for a jaw-dropping combination. Just ask Job. Here was a guy just like us. Someone who desired to follow God. Someone who was familiar with both blessing and hardship. Someone who found God and His ways a major slippery-fish experience— and decided to tell God exactly that.

Not only did Job flat out tell God that he didn't think He was playing fair, Job demanded that the Almighty account for His actions. That's when the unthinkable happened. God showed up.

I have to admit that I love the last five chapters of the Book of Job. It makes for great mental theatre. Here's the Almighty answering Job's whys with a list of whats—here's what I, the Lord, have created and you, Job, haven't:

> *"Where were you when I laid the foundations of the earth? Tell me, if you know so much. Do you know how its dimensions were determined and who did the surveying? What supports its foundations, and who laid its cornerstone as the morning stars sang together and all the angels shouted for joy?... Can you hold back the movements of the stars? Are you able to restrain the Pleiades or Orion? Can you ensure the proper sequence of the seasons or guide the constellation of the Bear with*

her cubs across the heavens? Do you know the laws of the universe and how God rules the earth? Can you shout to the clouds and make it rain? Can you make lightning appear and cause it to strike as you direct it? Who gives intuition and instinct? Who is wise enough to count all the clouds?"
—Job 38:4–7, 31–37 (NLT)

It's like God's telling Job, "Set your mind on whatever is lovely. That will tell you all you need to know."

As for Job's response? I picture Job going from self-righteous to self-conscious in record time. Talk about a big God, small brain moment! Job humbly replies,

"I was talking about things I did not understand, things far too wonderful for me... I had heard about you before, but now I have seen you with my own eyes. I take back everything I said, and I sit in dust and ashes to show my repentance."
— Job 42:3, 5–6 (NLT)

Though Job mentions having seen God with his own eyes, Scripture states that Job heard the voice of God in a storm or whirlwind. Nothing is mentioned about a face-to-face encounter. What Job *had* seen was God's handiwork. The loveliness of God's creation confirmed the truth of God's words in a way that allowed Job to more clearly "see" the Almighty, the invisible God.

Like Job, setting our minds on whatever is lovely helps us better understand who, and how big, God really is. At the same time, it reminds us of who, and how small, we really are. Lovely thoughts point us toward the path of humility.

But the Book of Job holds yet another touchstone to humility and loveliness. In Job 42:10, we learn that God restores Job's fortunes and even doubles them after their encounter. But something significant takes place before that happens. Verse 10 begins, *"When Job prayed for his friends."* Job's fortunes were restored after he prayed for the so-called friends who originally came to comfort him, but wound up doing anything but. Instead of providing support, they had torn Job down as they lectured, accused, and argued.

In turn, Job did something lovely. We don't know whether God (off the record) suggested Job pray for his spiritually nearsighted companions or if Job's brush with divinity and humility filled him with compassion and empathy. What we do know is that Job spoke to God on behalf of those who'd hurt him. That's when the things that had fallen apart started coming back together.

Job's intercessory prayer brings us back to God's self-declared favorite masterpiece: people. Nature is stunning, amazing, and altogether lovely. But people, well, we are in a class by ourselves. Ephesians 2:10 (NLT) declares, *"We are God's masterpiece."* In Greek, the kind of "master work" described in this verse is something made by a creator or poet. That makes us God's living, breathing poetry. Personally, I find that thought incredibly lovely.

In setting our minds on whatever is lovely, we cannot forget to include people. All kinds of people. Those we view as poetry, as well as those we may feel more inclined to classify as low-life limericks. Every individual bears something of incomparable loveliness, the image of God.

In His Image

Right from the start, Genesis 1, we can tell there is something different about God's final work of creation. God has just divided night from day, made sequoias and saguaros, koalas and kinkajous. Then, He says, *"Let us make human beings in our image, make them reflecting our nature"* (Genesis 1:26 *The Message*).

Out of all of God's incredible creations, we're the only ones who've been given this divine family resemblance. We alone bear the likeness of God. When we reflect on the truth of Romans 1:20, we cannot overlook the fact that God's invisible qualities, His eternal power and divine nature, can be seen not only in wonders like the Grand Canyon, but in people like you and me.

But what does it really mean to be created in God's image? Does it mean we're God's spitting image, like some kids are of their parents? Does God have two arms, two legs, and bad hair days? Since we are physical beings and God is "something else," we can be fairly certain that we don't bear His true image in terms of appearance. That means if we're looking for evidence of what God is like in ourselves or others, appearance is the first thing we can disregard. Now, there's something easier said than done, at least for us human folk. And that includes God's prophets.

In 1 Samuel 16, God is directing His prophet, Samuel, to anoint a new leader to take Saul's place as king over Israel. God even gives Samuel a hint as to this future king's identity: the leader will be one of the sons of Jesse. Enter Eliab, Jesse's eldest, and apparently buffest, son. 1 Samuel 16:6–7 says,

> *Samuel saw Eliab and thought, "Surely the LORD's anointed stands here before the LORD." But the LORD said to Samuel, "Do not consider his appearance or his height, for I have rejected him. The LORD does not look at the outward appearance, but the LORD looks at the heart."*
> —1 Samuel 16:6–7

Samuel did what we so often do. He made the mistake of judging a book by its cover, or in this case, a king by his frame. In contrast, God saw the true masterpiece within Jesse's youngest son, David. He saw the loveliness of his heart.

We are God's masterpieces. But our physical bodies are simply frames that display God's works of art. Like the world around us, the physical frames God chooses to use are evidence of His artist's heart. They show His love of diversity. Not only do people have different colors of skin and hair and eyes, we come in different sizes, shapes, and weights—just like artwork in a gallery. When artwork is on display, the size of its frame, and whether that frame is made of dark oak or light pine, painted, carved, gilded, or varnished, does not determine the value of the artwork itself. A frame's only job is to help display the masterpiece to its best advantage. The same is true for people.

Our artistic God, who so carefully laid the foundations of the earth, has chosen a unique frame for each of us. The psalmist says this about His creation of each of us:

> *"You created my inmost being; you knit me together in my mother's womb. I praise you because I am fearfully and wonderfully made; your works are wonderful, I know that full well. My frame was not hidden from you when I was made in the secret place. When I was woven together in the depths of the earth, your eyes saw my unformed body."*
> —Psalm 139:13–15

Yes, our frames are miraculous. They may even be considered beautiful. But they are not the source of mankind's innate loveliness. There's something else, something the rest of creation doesn't have. I believe that something is unconditional love. That's God's clearest fingerprint. His most accurate image. I believe our *"God [who] is love"* (1 John 4:16) could imprint nothing less on those whom He's chosen to bear His image.

Then why do we seem to consistently bear it so poorly? We were created in God's image, but we are not a self-portrait of Him. Only Jesus has that distinction. Isaiah 53:2 describes our Savior as having *"no beauty or majesty to attract us to him, nothing in his appearance that we should desire him."* It wasn't Jesus's frame that attracted people to Him. It was His love.

This same loveliness is innate within us. But we are works

in progress, masterpieces in the making. We're not complete yet. We're like those paintings beneath the tent in Scottsdale. When the artist begins a new creation, those watching see nothing but a few faintly penciled-in guidelines, followed by splotches of black, white, and gray. The canvas appears to be more messy chaos than masterpiece. But as time passes, and as the artist is allowed to continue his work, an image begins to emerge—an entire riverbed of stream-tumbled stones comes to light. For the audience, it's a delightful surprise, how those seemingly meaningless blobs of color became rocks and a running stream. For the artist, there's simply the satisfaction of a job well done. In his mind's eye, the artist had seen what the painting would look like long before the last brushstroke was made.

The Message explains God's artistry in creating us this way:

> *"God knew what he was doing from the very beginning. He decided from the outset to shape the lives of those who love him along the same lines as the life of his Son. The Son stands first in the line of humanity he restored. We see the original and intended shape of our lives there in him."*
> —Romans 8:29

We are all unique masterpieces in different stages of completion. Yet we all share something in common: We were originally designed to be conformed to the image of Christ. Again, that image has nothing to do with being physically shaped into a Jewish man with a beard. It has everything to do with the spiritual maturing of our hearts. Whatever is lovely may help draw us toward a *philéo* kind of love—that of a deep, enduring friendship—but it's God's Spirit that leads us even deeper into *agape* love, that unconditional, sacrificial love Christ has shown us. How clearly Christ's image is evident in our lives will depend on how willing we are to allow God to continue working on the masterpiece of us.

The further along the masterpiece, the more its loveliness will be revealed.

Lovely hearts do lovely things—like pray for those who've hurt them. They also seem to see lovely things more easily in the world, and in the people, around them. I'm not talking about having a Pollyanna view of life where we turn a blind eye toward evil. That kind of attitude certainly doesn't describe the Christ we see in the Gospels. But those who continue to grow in their love of God and others seem able to find whatever is lovely in the most unexpected places.

The Good, the Bad, and the Ugly

Let's head back to God's gallery for awhile. So far, we've viewed some amazing works of art. We've looked at the intrinsic loveliness God's imprinted into His creation, both in nature and in His masterpiece of people. We've been humbled by God's eternal power as we listened in on God's conversation with Job. We've caught a glimpse of God's divine nature as we studied His artist's heart, revealed through the beauty, detail, diversity, and organization of the works of His hands. But it's time we ventured into a brand-new wing of His gallery, one where we may not care to linger.

When I talk about exploring a different wing of God's gallery, what do I mean? Picture a real art museum. Say we've decided to hang out in the Monet section. We love it here. We enjoy it so much that we've decided we never really want to see anything else. After all, from our vantage point, everything's downright lovely. We've grown accustomed to the impressionist brushstrokes of blues, purples, and greens, to the landscapes of genteel country life and ponds filled with water lilies. If anyone asks us what "art" is like, we'll describe what we've experienced—Monets. "And what's the artist like?" He likes florals and oils and quiet, peaceful things.

But the Monets are only one wing of this gallery. Suppose one day we venture outside our little Monet comfort zone. We turn a corner and came face-to-face with a Picasso for the very first time. Bold lines. Reds. Yellows. Black. Everything looks cockeyed and crazy. We're not even sure what the image we're looking at is supposed to be. At this point, our confused little hearts would undoubtedly cry out, "That's not art!"

But what if we discovered that the same artist who painted the Monets also painted the Picassos. We'd either declare, "This is not the artist I know" and run back to the safety of our precious Monets or we'd sit down and take a closer look. If we decided to risk staying a while, and diligently searched for whatever is lovely in the works, it would be helpful if the artist joined us. We could ask him questions and express our own ignorance and uncertainty. All of our whys may not find immediate answers, but in time we might begin to see a glimpse of loveliness where before we saw only chaos. And who knows? One day we might even find ourselves remarking to someone else, perhaps a fellow Monet lover, "I've found there's a playful joy in Picassos."

One thing about art is that it's so subjective. We usually judge how good an artist is by whether or not the artist's finished piece suits our own personal taste. If we're not careful, we may find ourselves doing the exact same thing with God. We may applaud God's goodness when we view a weeping willow, a waterfall, or a whale. But what about poison ivy, scorpions, and hurricanes? We may agree God's image can surely be found in those who are kind and good and loving. But what about in mass murderers, pedophiles, and prostitutes?

When it comes to God, it's appealing to spend our lives in one small wing of His gallery—the wing that displays what we comprehend and agree with. This wing feels safe and comfortable. It suits our own personal taste and holds everything we've categorized as lovely. But I believe God's definition of *loveliness* is so much broader, and more eternal, than this.

Look at the Apostle Paul. In 2 Corinthians 12:7–10, he writes about receiving *"a thorn in the flesh,"* some type of physical ailment given to him to help keep him from becoming conceited. Three times Paul asks God to remove it. Yet the thorn remains. Instead of complaining, Paul turns to praising. He expounds on how this weakness allows God's power to better shine through his life. He sums it up by saying, "I delight in weaknesses, in insults, in hardships, in persecutions, in difficulties. For when I am weak, then I am strong."

This is more than having a "glass half-full" attitude. Here Paul ventures outside the gallery of physical, emotional, and relational comfort and discovers something lovely, something that drew Paul closer to God and other people closer to God through Paul. Paul's thorn became a touchstone to loveliness.

Wounds, pain, grief, struggle, hardship...these are not the kinds of artwork we care to gaze at for long. But maybe we should. Sure, some of it comes from living in a fallen world. Some of it is not the work of God's hands, but the consequences of free will flailing in the hands of sinful people and Satan's twisted attempts at vandalizing the glory of God's gallery.

Sometimes, the only way to tell who the true creator is behind something is to go on a mental treasure hunt for whatever is lovely. We may need to sit with what we consider ugly for awhile, studying the deep shadows and running our fingers along the rough edges. We may feel repulsed, frightened, or confused. But we never sit alone. God is with us in every wing of His gallery as both our Curator and Creator. He's there to help us learn to spot the difference between a masterpiece and a forgery. He's waiting to open our eyes to more and more loveliness as our hearts become more like His.

Deep "C" Fishing

The ancient Celts believed there were "thin places" on this earth, locations where the boundary between heaven and earth was blurred. The more we set our minds on things above, the more we'll recognize that we live our lives in a "thin place" where the spiritual realm is constantly intersecting with our physical world. Loveliness is one of the boundary stones between God's kingdom and our earthly home. It points the way toward who God is and who He wants us to be. Let's follow its lead a bit further.

1. In Psalm 84:1, the Hebrew word for *lovely* is used to describe God's dwelling place. Though God actually dwells everywhere, the following verses of Scripture describe heaven, the place we regard as God's home—and our future dwelling place. Read Psalm 84:1 and 103:19; and Revelation 7:9–17; 21:1–4, 22–27; and 22:1–5.

• Name a few things that make God's dwelling place lovely. How is heaven different from our home here on earth? What do heaven and earth have in common?

Second Corinthians 5:5 in *The Message* says,
> *"We've been given a glimpse of the real thing, our true home, our resurrection bodies! The Spirit of God whets our appetite by giving us a taste of what's ahead. He puts a little of heaven in our hearts so that we'll never settle for anything less."*

- How does setting your mind on whatever is lovely whet your appetite for heaven?

2. In this chapter, we looked at Romans 8:29, which talks about how God's purpose for us is to be conformed to the image of His Son. The verse directly before this, Romans 8:28, says, *"We know that in all things God works for the good of those who love him, who have been called according to his purpose."*

- How can having a lovely, Christlike heart enable us to better see the good God is working in all things?

- How can unconditional love help us recognize loveliness in others? How can being wholeheartedly loved and accepted by someone else help open our own eyes to the masterpiece God is completing in us?

- Choose a touchstone that will remind you to look for loveliness in others, particularly those whom you view as Picassos in a Monet world.

3. Time for an art project. Don't panic! Even if you don't consider yourself artistic, you can create something lovely. Take some photos. Play with watercolors. Write a song. Cook a meal for someone in need. Plant a garden. Write a note telling a friend some of the lovely things you've seen God do through him or her. Then, spend some time with God talking about what you experienced during the process of creation.

- How did it feel to be a "creator"? What is lovely about your creation? What does creating something teach you about the One who created you?

- Take a "spiritual field trip" to a park or anywhere you can surround yourself with God's creation. (Don't forget to pack your Bible and a bottle of water.) Find somewhere comfortable where you can sit and read the last five chapters of Job. After you've finished, walk through your chosen wing of God's gallery and share your heart with the Artist. You may want to pick up a rock as a touchstone along the way to remind you of what you and God talked about together.

CHAPTER NINE

THE POWER OF A GOOD WORD

"Whatever is admirable."
—Philippians 4:8

Just last night on the news, I heard that Britney Spears had been the number one topic searched for on Yahoo!— a distinction she had apparently held for six years straight. Similarly on eBay, Britney-related items outsold all others, with more than 34,000 different items successfully bid on in the 12 months. These treasures included cigarette butts, chewed gum, and the Red Bull can Britney was holding when she had her head shaved. Apparently bids have declined as a result of all the bad press the pop princess has received. One year, Britney's half-eaten egg salad sandwich and a corn dog munched on by her then husband Kevin Federline sold as a "twofer" for $520. The next year, the 34,345 items only generated about $34,000 total.

So why do we care? That's a good question. Proverbs 18:8 (TNIV) tells us that *"the words of a gossip are like choice morsels; they go down to the inmost parts."* They also sell a lot of magazines, advertising, records, books, movie tickets, and, apparently, prechewed gum. In the paraphrased version in *The Message*, Proverbs 18:8 compares listening to gossip to *"eating cheap candy,"* then asks, *"Do you really want junk like that in your belly?"* The question Philippians 4:8 asks us is, "Do we really want junk like that in our minds?"

The Watering Hole of Words

A few years back, researchers at Duke University conducted a study with rhesus macaques—monkeys. These monkeys were given the choice between a big drink of cherry juice or a small sip of juice accompanied by the opportunity to look at a photo of a socially dominant member of their primate group. It seems that cherry juice to a rhesus monkey is like a Caramel Macchiato with double whipped cream to many of the humans I know. But over and over again, the monkeys chose to curb their cherry juice intake so they could check out the photo of a local celebrity

I can relate to these monkeys. I'm drawn to reading *People* magazine (and as a human, I can choose to indulge in a *venti* Caramel Macchiato along with it). My favorite articles are about people I've never heard of before, individuals who've triumphed in the face of great odds or who've dedicated their lives to making a difference in the world. But that doesn't mean I pass by the photos of the rich and famous. I've been known to linger over the outrageous fashions and tell-all photos of who's had something lifted, shifted, or removed. Like a monkey, I'm drawn to check out those in the spotlight.

But monkeys have one advantage over me in this area. They can't talk. While "monkey see, monkey do" may hold true, "monkey see, monkey gossip" isn't going to happen. "Vicki see, Vicki gossip" is another matter. It's obvious that if I spread rumors or make derogatory comments about people within my circle of family and friends, damage can be done. But, what about Britney or Lindsay or Paris? If I talk about people I'll never cross paths with, people who will never be hurt personally by my words, what's the harm?

"People can tame all kinds of animals, birds, reptiles, and fish, but no one can tame the tongue. It is an uncontrollable evil, full of deadly poison. Sometimes it praises our Lord and Father, and sometimes it breaks out into curses against those who have been made in the image of God. And so blessing and cursing come pouring out of the same mouth. Surely, my brothers and sisters, this is not right! Does a spring of water bubble out with both fresh water and bitter water? Can you pick olives from a fig tree or figs from a grapevine? No, and you can't draw fresh water from a salty pool."
—James 3:7–12 (NLT)

Just call me Old Salty. For years I asked God to help me control what came out of my mouth, because, frankly, I talk a lot and sometimes it can get me in trouble. But over time God has shown me that when I blurt something out that embarrasses me or that I feel guilty over later, that's a good thing. Every word I speak is a touchstone that reveals the health of my heart. Inappropriate words are my warning signal that something's amiss. What comes out of my mouth lets me (and those around me) know what lies at my very core—a spring of living water or a stagnant, brackish pool.

But surely I can cut myself a little slack. According to God's Word my tongue and my heart seem to be in cahoots to make sure I fail in this area. Right before admonishing me to praise and bless instead of curse, James 3 plainly states, *"No one can tame the tongue."* To make matters worse, Jeremiah 17:9 declares, *"The heart is deceitful above all things and beyond cure."* So what's a *People*-loving girl to do?

Draw close to God and remember these promises: I've been given a new heart and spirit (Ezekiel 11:19); I'm a new creation (2 Corinthians 5:17); I've been born again (John 3:7; 1 Peter 1:23); I've died to sin (Romans 6:2); I have the mind of Christ (1 Corinthians 2:16). I am not who I once was! I've had a heart, spirit, and even a *mind* transplant. And my words should reflect that fact.

But once again, I forget. It's like when my daughter, Katrina, got married. The family name she was most closely identified with changed. Katrina left the home of her father and me to begin a new life with her husband, Ryan. As a touchstone of this monumental change, Katrina changed her last name from Kuyper to Fink. After two years, I still have lapses when I introduce her as Katrina Kuyper. I know better, but old habits die hard.

The same is true when it comes to my old identity. The way I think, the actions I take, and the words I speak sometimes fall back into patterns I acquired during the first two decades of my life. Back before I was born again. It's like a zombie resurrected in *The Night of the Living Dead*. Only this time it's *The Night of the Dead, Living*. What died with Christ has burst back up from the grave. Talk about a horror film!

I can't repeat it enough. (Because if you're anything like me, you've forgotten it already.) This is the reason why consistently setting our minds on things above, as we're exhorted to do in Colossians 3:2, is so important. Though Colossians 3:2 tells us *what* to do, it's the verses that surround it, Colossians 3:1 and 3, that reveal the *why*:

> *"Since, then, you have been raised with Christ, set your hearts on things above, where Christ is seated at the right hand of God. Set your minds on things above, not on earthly things. For you died, and your life is now hidden with Christ in God."*
> —Colossians 3:1–3

MONKEY SEE, MONKEY DO

So…how does setting our minds on whatever is admirable help us remember we're alive in Christ, while at the same time keeping us dead to our former, self-centered habits? By paying attention to who we admire, and why, we can discover a lot about what's going on in our heads and hearts—with whom, and what, we are truly identifying.

The Greek word that the NIV translates as "admirable" in Philippians 4:8 varies with almost every major translation of the Bible. It appears as "commendable," "honorable," "reputable," "respectable," and "of good report," to list a few. But the gist remains the same. We are to set our minds on what we can speak well of, on what is positive and constructive, instead of negative and destructive. *The Living Bible* expands on this by telling us to *"dwell on the fine, good things in others."* Obviously, gossip reveals we've been doing the exact opposite.

At first glance, linking those we admire with gossip may seem incongruous. After all, gossip isn't about admiration. It's about cattiness and contempt, right? Not always. When we gossip, we simply use someone else's story—whether true, exaggerated, or fabricated—to our own advantage, because our own story doesn't seem grand enough, or entertaining enough, to share with those around us. Sometimes, we cut others down, making them seem smaller, in the hope we'll appear larger. Sometimes, we link our own story to the story of someone we admire to make ourselves seem more admirable by association. Either way, this kind of gossip is the tasty morsel that makes us feel "full" of ourselves.

But gossip's choice morsels don't stop there. The reason gossip reaches our "inmost parts," what other versions of the Bible often translate as our *heart*, is because we have made a heart connection with the people we gossip about. We're interested in them—their successes, failures, and faux pas. We may admire them outright or claim to despise them. But either way we've built a relationship with them, even if we just "hang out" together in our minds. Those we hang out with, we often envy—and emulate.

Young children learn by watching their parents. As adults, our tendency to follow in the footsteps of others doesn't come to an abrupt halt. In our search for role models and heroes, for someone to lead us toward something greater than ourselves, some of our examples may cross over and become idols.

Our hearts were designed for worship. If God is not filling that rightful spot, something or someone else will. Celebrities often fit that bill. By definition, a celebrity is someone we "celebrate." Someone we idolize. Someone we put on a pedestal, because that person seems to have something the rest of us don't. Something we kinda wish we could claim as our own.

We may not physically bow down to these people, but fans tend to "fan"-tasize. The more we watch, read, and listen to details about the lives of those we choose to shower our admiration on, the more time we spend with them. The stronger the mental connections are that we build with them, the greater chance there is that we will be inclined to "walk" just like them. Modern culture bears witness to the fact that imitation is often our sincerest form of flattery. It's why fashion trends and slang terms can spread faster than a flu bug in a preschool. But it's our attitudes, more than our apparel, that is most at risk. Proverbs 13:20 (*The Message*) says, "*Become wise by walking with the wise; hang out with fools and watch your life fall to pieces.*"

If God's purpose for our lives is for us to be conformed to the image of Christ, the people we choose to admire, and how high a pedestal we put them on, matters. It can make a difference in the way we walk—and the way we talk.

Spoken into Being

There is something about words that God holds very close to His heart. The Gospel of John begins with this statement: "*In the beginning was the Word, and the Word was with God, and the Word was God. He was with God in the beginning. Through him all things were made*" (1:1–3). God names His Son "the Word." And it is the Word through which everything in this universe and beyond was made.

God chose to communicate to us through the Word and His words, through Christ and the Bible. We communicate with God through words in prayer. And when it comes to being created in God's image, I believe words are one more way (in addition to sharing unconditional love) that we bear a resemblance to our heavenly Father.

If we compare men and women with the rest of God's creation, we notice that we are the only ones who use words. Some animals may communicate on a very simple level, but this ability doesn't really venture into the world of words and ideas, of connecting on a relational level. We don't all speak the same language, and some of us may even speak with our hands instead of our vocal chords, but we all have a drive to communicate with one another, to impart information, to share hopes and dreams, to build relationships. I believe we speak because God does—because we are created in His likeness. If this is true, if our speech is one way we reflect God's image, we need to take a closer look at what comes out of our mouths.

The Bible tells us that God regards words as both sacred and powerful. That's one reason using God's name in a derogatory way or breaking a marriage vow is such a serious matter to Him. Words matter. In the Sermon on the Mount, Jesus speaks in the same breath about murderers and those who berate others verbally. Words have the power to wound or heal, to cut, or to cleanse. And we often banter them about so carelessly.

A while back, a friend of mine shared how shocked he was at the words that came out of his mouth when he was angry with his wife. This is a man who deeply loves God and his spouse, and honestly desires to honor them both with his lips. His self-diagnosis was a lack of self-control. He said, "If only I had better self-control, I could be the man God wants me to be and the husband my wife needs me to be."

It's true—self-control is a fruit of the Spirit. But it's not the key to living a godly life. If it were, we wouldn't need the New Covenant—or Christ. We can encourage this fruit to mature by tilling the soil it grows in. We can be intentional about becoming more disciplined in our lives. We can ask others to hold us accountable so we'll become more aware of habits we need to change. We can pray. But growth is the work of God's hands, not ours. It's our heart, not our habits, that holds the key to speaking good words.

Matthew 12:34 says, *"For out of the overflow of the heart the mouth speaks."* *The Message* paraphrases this same verse (and the two that follow it) in these words:

> *"It's your heart, not the dictionary, that gives meaning to your words. A good person produces good deeds and words season after season. An evil person is a blight on the orchard. Let me tell you something: Every one of these careless words is going to come back to haunt you. There will be a time of Reckoning. Words are powerful; take them seriously. Words can be your salvation. Words can also be your damnation."*

As I mentioned before, words are kind of like verbal EKGs. They reveal the health of our hearts sometimes before we're even aware there's a problem. Pity the poor celebrities whose words are played over and over again for everyone to hear. It seems that almost weekly someone of note is making a public apology about something he or she said but "didn't really mean." The truth is that our words, especially what we say in our most unguarded or emotional moments, often reveal hidden stashes of things like impurity, selfishness, prejudice, or pride. Believe it or not, that's good news.

If we aren't aware of a problem, chances are it won't get fixed. It's like a car that starts making a funny noise. If we're paying attention, that funny noise should send us straight to the mechanic to have things checked out. (Unless you happen to be mechanically inclined enough to attempt to fix it yourself, which I'm not.) Without that noisy, telltale sign of trouble, we could find ourselves stalled somewhere along the highway in the not-so-distant future.

Setting our minds on what is admirable and commendable is kind of like a tune-up for our hearts. As we choose to dwell on the fine, good things in others, we reinforce our search for whatever is lovely. But then we move one step further. We let whatever is lovely overflow from our lips. We choose to give a good report about others. We commend what is commendable.

But if our hearts are still a work in progress and we find ourselves dumbstruck, if the only words that come to mind would be fodder for the rumor mill or words that will hurt instead of heal, we do have another option. We can focus our words upward instead of outward.

THE LANGUAGE OF PRAYER

In a nutshell, prayer is communication with God. But it's so much richer than casual conversation. It can be a plea for help; an outpouring of awe; a heaven-bound thank-you note. It can be questions and confusion and ramblings and *"groans that words cannot express"* (Romans 8:26). It can also be a touchstone to help us set our minds on whatever is admirable.

Mom always said, "If you can't find anything nice to say about someone, don't say anything at all." That's good advice in terms of tempering our tongues. But instead of letting those unsaid words simmer in our hearts and minds, prayer gives us the opportunity to help change a bad report into a good one.

Jesus explains:

> *"You're familiar with the old written law, 'Love your friend,' and its unwritten companion, 'Hate your enemy.' I'm challenging that. I'm telling you to love your enemies. Let them bring out the best in you, not the worst. When someone gives you a hard time, respond with the energies of prayer, for then you are working out of your true selves, your God-created selves."*
> —Matthew 5:43–44 *(The Message)*

It's easy to pray for those we love. Our care and concern for those close to our heart lovingly shapes our prayers into pleas for their health and happiness, their protection and prosperity. But praying for the good of those who've wronged us, or even for those who simply rub us the wrong way, is more of a chore and less of a joy. Our cry for "justice" shouts louder than God's call to "mercy." In the Sermon on the Mount, Jesus says, *"Blessed are the merciful, for they will be shown mercy"* (Matthew 5:7). An intercessory prayer for the good of someone we cannot wholeheartedly give a "good report" about is more than merciful. It can be miraculous.

How prayer works, well...that's definitely a slippery-fish aspect of God for me. All I know is that God tells me to pray. He promises both to listen and to answer. Sometimes, circumstances change. Sometimes, they don't. I know there's a whole freewill issue involved when we pray for other people, but I'm familiar enough with God to know how powerful and creative He is. (Remember the cow's eyeball?) I'm sure God can provide plenty of opportunities for others to change their heart, their life, and the trajectory of their eternity—and somehow my little prayers can help. Exactly how that happens is all a little fuzzy.

But one thing I know for sure. Prayer changes me. It changes my attitudes, my perspective, my desires, and ultimately, my own heart. And somewhere along the way, it changes the way I think.

I used to joke about my habit of buying *People* magazine to read on long plane trips. I told others I could really relax when I read it "because there aren't even people in here I feel obligated to pray for." That's changed. *People* magazine has actually become a touchstone to prayer for me. Often, I find myself praying for those whose lives are envied by so many yet who seem to possess so little of eternal worth. Praying for those I used to make fun of or idolize for all the wrong reasons has cleansed some of the cattiness from my soul. It's hard to gossip about people you're praying for.

As I mentioned before, those we despise, as well as those we admire, we hang out with in our heads. We build relational bonds that can lead us to follow in their footsteps. As we pray for whatever is admirable to grow in the lives of others, we also build relational bonds with those we're praying for. But this time, those bonds are positive. They can help us work the kinks out of our true selves, our God-created selves, as mentioned in Matthew 5.

You don't need to follow in my meandering footsteps by using *People* magazine to remind you to pray for the growth of fine, good things in others. There are plenty of other touchstones to choose from. Simply fire up your imagination and follow in God's creative footsteps. A simple prayer list of names works for some people. However, if you're a visual learner, you could create a prayer scrapbook. Instead of adding names to a prayer list, put photos in a self-adhesive album—or business cards, Christmas cards, even clippings from *People* magazine.

Personally, I'm a musical learner. Hearing familiar songs can instantly send my mind back to a specific time, place, or person. So, I use that quirk as a resource for audio touchstones to prayer. For instance, while driving near Taos, New Mexico, I stopped for an impromptu worship service by the side of the road in the shadow of a magnificent vista of rocky cliffs. I was soon joined by a young man with a Rastafarian hairdo, as exuberant about sharing his appreciation of the view as I was. We chitchatted a bit about how much he enjoyed living in nearby Angel Fire but how difficult it was to find a job. When I asked what the young man's dream job would be, he said he wanted to be a spiritual healer. I inquired a bit further as to what that entailed, when the young man turned to me and said, "I can tell you are a spiritual person. Are you married?" A bit taken aback, I replied, "Over 20 wonderful years!" At that, the young man shot both arms straight up into the air and shouted at the top of his lungs, "Yes! That's what I want! I knew true love could still be found!"

At that point, the young man's friend called him back to their truck and we said our good-byes. As I got back in my Bug, the song "I Can See Clearly Now" by Johnny Nash came on the radio. I began praying that the man I just met would be able to see God clearly, that he would find the love he was looking for, that he would lead an admirable life. That was over five years ago, but whenever I hear that song I pray for the stranger I met along the road that day. Without the help of Johnny Nash, I doubt that young man would ever cross my mind. But I believe my prayers can go farther than my conversation ever had a chance to. They're one small gift I'm happy to give to those I admire—and to those I wish I could.

THE WORDS WE GIVE AWAY

Gossip isn't the only tasty morsel around. Proverbs 18:20–21 (*The Message*) tells us that *"words satisfy the mind as much as fruit does the stomach; good talk is as gratifying as a good harvest. Words kill, words give life; they're either poison or fruit—you choose."* Good words are health food for our minds. When we share them with others we feast together. And when we verbally extol what is admirable and commendable in someone else, we pass on a touchstone, something that person may treasure for years.

One of the most powerful verbal touchstones anyone has ever given to me was a one-sentence gift from a stranger. I was at a restaurant, a rather upscale eatery that boasted a magnificent view. My dining companion that day was my grandmother, who was in her 90s and had dementia. Every three or four minutes we would run through the same conversation. My grandmother would say, "Where am I?"

And I'd reply, "We're out at a restaurant today. Isn't the view pretty? Look at the mountains!"

Then she'd ask, "How am I going to pay for this?"

I'd tell her, "Don't worry, it's all taken care of. You have enough money to pay your bills and I'm treating for lunch today."

She'd continue with something like, "You should just throw me in the gutter! I'm no good anymore."

And I'd try to reassure her with, "I love you, Grandma. I know some days feel really hard, but I'm glad you're here. Look at the mountains!"

"Where am I?...How am I going to pay for this?" And so on.

On this particular day, my grandmother and I had the good fortune of having the restaurant virtually to ourselves. The only other patron was a businessman, sitting by himself and reading a newspaper as he ate his lunch. Unfortunately, the waiter seated us directly behind him. As my grandmother and I waited for our own lunch to arrive, time seemed to drag. Our conversation repeated itself over and over again like an old LP with a scratch in it. The whole time, I was uncomfortably aware of this poor businessman who had undoubtedly come up to this restaurant over his limited lunch break to enjoy a little peace and quiet.

When our lunch finally arrived, my grandmother took one look at it and said, "I'm not hungry." My heart sank as my frustration level rose. Just then, the businessman stood up to leave. But instead of walking by, he stopped at our table and knelt down to look me in the eye. I was petrified, ready to receive a tongue lashing like a parent whose unruly child has disrupted another patron's good time. Instead, this stranger said in the kindest, most gentle tone, "When I get older, I hope I have a granddaughter just like you." Then, he smiled and walked out the door.

I hung onto those words tightly for the next few years. They lifted my heart, reassuring me that my efforts weren't wasted, as I watched my grandmother fade from this life into the next. They also gave me a second wind when six weeks after my maternal grandmother died, my paternal grandmother moved to town. For the last six years of my paternal grandmother's life, this stranger's words helped me persevere. They gave me hope.

"Say only what helps, each word a gift," Ephesians 4:29 (*The Message*) tells us. This stranger gave me a priceless gift. He didn't have to say anything to me. He could have walked right on by and never given my grandmother and me a second thought. But this man took the time to give a "good report." And though I don't know this man personally, I believe I know something about him. I believe he has a good heart, one that overflows with good words.

If a total stranger can choose the perfect verbal gift for me, imagine what we can give to those we know and love. By sharing a good report of whatever is lovely, the glimpse of God's image we catch reflected in others, we may be able to help those around us see God's image more clearly in themselves. Our words can serve as touchstones to help others set their minds more firmly on things above.

Although sharing our praise and encouragement aloud is always important, commending someone through the written word creates a touchstone that others can hold in their hands, instead of simply in their heart. I actually keep a treasure chest of thank-you notes and encouraging letters I've received. When I feel depressed or discouraged, I take time to reread a few of these written touchstones. They never fail to lift my mood and lead me back to thanking God for what He's done and for the people He's brought into my life.

When I was a new mom with two young children 18 months apart, I started something I dubbed Cold Water Ministries. Its inspiration came courtesy of Proverbs 25:25: *"Like cold water to a weary soul is good news from a distant land."* My goal was to write one letter each day, 30 letters a month, to people who could use a word of encouragement. I only continued this letter blitz for about a year, but if the letters I received in return are any indication, I believe my time was well spent.

Unfortunately, the invention of email, along with all the writing I do each day for my job, seems to have pretty much squelched my letter writing endeavors. (We won't even get started on what it's done to sending out Christmas cards.) And that's a shame. Email is quick and convenient—and not to be ignored as a viable way to send along a positive, commendable word. But "delete" happens so quickly. I think letter writing is not only a lost art, but a lost opportunity for ministry. Think of the impact the letters written by Christ's followers continue to have on us today.

Our words matter. Regardless of whether they're spoken, written, or whispered in that running commentary of thoughts that plays in our heads. Our words show us for who we really are. The more true, noble, right, pure, and lovely our words, the more commendable our hearts, and the more admirable the lives we'll lead.

Deep "C" Fishing

Whatever is admirable has a lot in common with *whatever is noble* and *whatever is lovely.* Some aspects of these concepts may overlap, but that doesn't make them repetitive. As a matter of fact, what we learn from setting our minds on any one of these topics could be a book in itself—a book that would take a lifetime to write. For now, let's just take some time to consider a few personal questions in the context of God's Word, perhaps picking up a touchstone or two along the way.

1. Matthew 6:21 (NLT) says, *"Wherever your treasure is, there your heart and thoughts will also be."*

• What does this verse have to say about who and what you think is admirable?

• How can you tell a true and lasting treasure from fool's gold?

- Write a prayerful list of what you truly treasure. Be honest. Then, make another list: If someone gauged what meant the most to you by how you spent your time and money, and by what you talked about most, what would that list of treasures look like?

- Are there any treasures you'd like to set aside or hold closer to your heart?

2. Good words are blessings, words that draw others toward God and toward the things He holds in high regard. They are words of life. Curses are simply words that draw people in the opposite direction, away from God and His abundant life. Read Deuteronomy 30:19 and consider the power of your words.

- How do you think the truth of this verse plays out in real life?

- Think of a verbal blessing you've received from someone else that has become a touchstone in your life. Why do you think it was so significant to you?

- Can you think of an example from your own life where someone has "cursed" you? Are you still holding on to those words as a touchstone? Ask God to help you lay them aside and pray for the good of the person who spoke those hurtful words to you.

- Write a letter to someone you admire this week. Commend that person for what you see in his or her life. Seal your touchstone with prayer before you deliver it.

3. Read one chapter of Proverbs each morning for the next month. Highlight every verse that relates to the words you speak. Choose at least one verse to memorize. Make a mental note of how frequently that verse comes to mind—and how it changes the words that come out of your mouth.

CHAPTER TEN

THE ROAD TO JOY

"If anything is excellent or praiseworthy."
—Philippians 4:8

I've got the joy, joy, joy, joy up in my brain. Where? Up in my brain. What? Up in my brain!" OK, so those aren't the original lyrics for that Sunday School classic. But maybe they should be. That's because what we choose to set our minds on not only affects how we act, but how we feel. And we like to feel good.

For years, whenever I felt my mood begin to spiral downward, I pursued a threefold road to recovery I called "cry, eat, and watch movies." First, I went off by myself. Well, almost by myself. I usually invited along my three personal therapists: Little Debbie, Ben, and Jerry. Then, I'd turn on a tearjerker movie so I could cry myself silly and blame my down-in-the-dumps feelings on the sappy plot instead of on my own personal problems. Those, I'd squish down a bit deeper below the surface. As a road to recovery goes, this one was not so effective. In reality, it was kind of like driving myself into an emotional ditch.

One day I decided to have a chat with my heavenly Father regarding my "cry, eat, and watch movies" approach to more balanced emotional health. Amazing as it seems, God showed me I was on the right track. I was doing exactly what He, the Great Physician, prescribed throughout the Old Testament. I simply needed to readjust my focus. To do that, I traded my movies for memories, and learned how to regularly celebrate what was *"excellent or praiseworthy."*

ADORATION THROUGH CELEBRATION

Over the course of the last six chapters, we've ventured out on quite the mental fishing trip. Now, as the Apostle Paul begins to wind up his list of brain-worthy topics, he throws out one final, all-encompassing net to encourage all of us forgetful, easily distracted fishermen to not give up fishing for what truly matters.

The phrase *"if anything is excellent or praiseworthy"* covers every aspect of who God is and what He's done. The word *excellence,* translated as "virtue" in the NKJV, describes a moral perfection that is both pleasing to God and promotes the ultimate good of mankind. As our lives and minds are conformed more and more to the image of Christ, glimmers of this God-generated excellence begin to glisten through us into the world around us—and our own personal stories begin to echo the storyline of God's epic tale of eternity. One way to help keep our thoughts attuned to whatever is excellent and praiseworthy is to set our minds more frequently on this ongoing story—a story worth hearing, worth telling, worth remembering, and worth celebrating.

When something is praiseworthy, our obvious response should be to give praise. But (need I say it yet again?) we forget. Obviously, this was just as much an Old Testament problem as it is a modern-day struggle. That's one reason why, way back in Leviticus, God gave His children a template for an amazingly adaptable touchstone to help them better remember the story they are a part of. That touchstone was celebration.

Back in Old Testament times, God decreed several annual celebrations. The "big three" festivals for the people of Israel (which after the Temple was completed traditionally included a pilgrimage to Jerusalem) began with the Passover, which was held in the spring and began the weeklong Feast of Unleavened Bread. This festival commemorated the Israelites' escape from Egypt and God's protection of their firstborn sons when the angel of death "passed over" their homes.

Fifty days after Passover, God instructed the Israelites to celebrate Pentecost. Many people think that this festival was in honor of Moses receiving the Book of the Law from God on Mount Sinai. Pentecost also began the Feast of Weeks, which celebrated the beginning of the grain harvest and was a time for remembering God's bounty.

In the late fall, the Feast of Tabernacles, which is also called the Festival of Booths, took place. During this celebration, the people of Israel built *sukkot*, which were temporary shelters constructed to resemble those the Israelites used during their journey toward the Promised Land. For one week each year, the Israelites ate their meals, entertained guests, and sometimes even slept, in their family's *sukkah*. During this time, they reflected on God's benevolent provision for the needs of His people during their 40 years in the desert.

These three festivals all had something in common. They all offered those partaking in the celebration a chance to cry, eat, and watch movies. OK, so my translation may vary a bit from the original Hebrew, but consider it in light of the Psalms.

Psalm 130:1 says, *"Out of the depths I cry to you, O Lord; O Lord, hear my voice."* This is just one example of someone "crying" out to God in the Bible. There are many others, including Jesus's prayerful cry to His Father at Gethsemane.

Prayer is our heart's purest cry. It can be a cry for help or a burst of praise. When the people of Israel held a sacred festival, they set aside their work for a predetermined time to focus on God. They spent some of that time crying out to God in prayer, in song, and with their sacrificial gifts.

But they not only cried—they also "ate." It's true that Jewish feast days often involved special foods, but here I'm talking about taking a big bite of God's word and chewing on it for awhile. Psalm 34:8 (NLT) encourages us to *"taste and see that the LORD is good,"* while 63:5 (NLT) notes, *"You* [meaning God] *satisfy me more than the richest of foods. I will praise you with songs of joy."*

Since the people of Israel didn't have their own copy of the Old Testament packed away in their camels' saddlebags, festivals were a special time when God's Word was read aloud in the presence of the whole community. Listening to God's Laws often sparked a time of mourning and repentance as God's people were confronted with how their lives had fallen short of what was pleasing to Him. But it was also a time for rejoicing and remembrance, as stories of God's faithfulness as He led His children out of Egypt were recounted.

This was where the lights dimmed and the movies began to roll. Psalm 77:11–12 from *The Message* says, *"Once again I'll go over and over what GOD has done, lay out on the table the ancient wonders; I'll ponder all the things you've accomplished, and give a long, loving look at your acts."*

When we remember what God has done—when we reminisce about what is excellent and praiseworthy—we run movies on the movie screen of our mind's eye. The story of what God did for the Israelites is one story that is replayed again and again throughout Scripture. Not only is it recorded in the Book of Exodus, it's recounted in Psalm 105, Psalm 106, Nehemiah 9, and Hebrews 11. That's because it's a story worth telling—and worth remembering.

Psalm 42:6 in *The Message* says, *"When my soul is in the dumps, I rehearse everything I know of you."* That's the true road to joy…a mental rehearsal of God's excellence, of His praiseworthy acts. That's what has the power to lead us out of our emotional wasteland and set our feet back on the solid rock of God's truth. Something a copy of *Steel Magnolias* and a pint of Ben and Jerry's can never do.

MOVIE MARATHON

There's another verse, Psalm 42:4, paraphrased in *The Message* that has helped paint a perfect word picture for me of this process: "*These are the things I go over and over, emptying out the pockets of my life.*" Just like our winter coats, the pockets of our lives get littered with odds and ends. The ticket stubs of broken promises. The crumpled tissues of disappointment and failure. The bent paper clips of angry words aimed at our hearts. How often do I absentmindedly toy with what should be discarded trash, rolling it around in my mental "fingers" for awhile?

Instead of rehearsing what I know about God, I begin to rehearse how I've been hurt and why I have a right to feel discouraged. That's a sure sign it's time to switch DVDs. That's because the movies we play in our minds help determine the landscape of our hearts. So often, we turn that around the opposite way. We allow our emotions to determine our actions and to influence what our minds will rest on for awhile.

The words *remember, recall,* and *ponder* appear over and over throughout the Book of Psalms. It seems the psalmists made a conscious effort to remember the good times. They recalled when God came through. They pondered not only what God had done in their lives, but throughout the history of the world as written in Scripture. They refocused their eyes on the big picture, on God's picture, and on their part in that picture. Then, they replayed that in their mind.

That's how we make something stick. We bring it to mind repeatedly until it begins popping up on its own when we need it most. We notice in the Book of Psalms that even if a psalm begins deep in despair, by the time it ends most psalmists are back to singing God's praises—even though their circumstances haven't changed.

We can take a lesson from the psalmists and the children of Israel. We can take time to mentally rehearse God's biblical blockbusters, as well as our own personal classics. But first we need to be aware of what they are. What would be your Top Ten all-time, God-came-through-for-me moments? Are you stumped or does your mind have a hard time stopping at just number 10? These don't have to be on par with parting the Red Sea or receiving a delivery of manna when the cupboard was bare. They're simply times when you caught sight, or briefly caught hold, of our slippery-fish God. They are moments that left you longing for more...more of things above.

This blockbuster moment could be the birth of a child, the death knell of an addiction, or the healing of a broken heart. It could be a long-awaited answer to prayer or an acute sense of God's presence when you needed it most. Not every blockbuster will be perfectly resolved like a movie of the week. Some may be a cliffhanger for a continuing series. But one common thread will tie them together. Somewhere in the story you will have glimpsed the excellence and praiseworthy character of the living God.

When was the last time you emptied the useless rubbish from the lint-filled corners of life's pockets and then entered the theater of remembrance to watch a great movie with the Lord? It's something that doesn't happen by chance. It's like getting together with an old friend. Unless you get out the calendar and make a date, the closest you'll get to doing it is talking about it. That is, if you don't forget about it all together when life gets hectic.

One thing I try to do at least twice a year is schedule a day away with God. I've found it's the perfect time to do a little pocket cleaning and movie viewing. My husband was actually the one who came up with the idea. For the last several years, he's regularly scheduled a day off work where he heads to a quiet, preferably picturesque spot outdoors. He takes his Bible, a notebook or journal, and a snack. He doesn't schedule any activities. He just hangs out with God.

The first year Mark tried this day away, he admitted to being a little anxious about what he'd do with all that time if God didn't show up. But, God did. And when Mark came home that evening, he said he could hardly believe how quickly the time had passed—and how refreshed and refocused he felt.

Although a full day away is wonderful, the length of time isn't as important as what we choose to set our minds on during that time. I usually begin by reading from the Book of Psalms. The whole of Scripture is well worth mentally munching on, but the psalms are so bite-sized and emotionally accessible. Our circumstances may differ, but the psalmists and I have a lot in common. We struggle. We rejoice. We get tired, discouraged, afraid, and confused. And on occasion, we intentionally choose to focus on the supreme excellence of God and respond by tossing verbal garlands of praise His way.

I have a system for reading the Book of Psalms that I fall back on anytime I'm in need of a spiritual oasis, whether during my day away or when my morning quiet times begin to feel a bit rote. Since there are 150 psalms and generally 30 (or 31) days in the month, I read 5 psalms a day. I begin by reading the psalm that coincides with the date. Since as I write this today is the 29th of the month, I would read Psalm 29. Then I add 30. That takes me to Psalm 59. Add 30 again, Psalm 89, then 119, and 149. Just take the date and keep adding 30.

After reading the Book of Psalms, I simply start talking to God about anything and everything. I may write a few psalms of my own or sing a few choruses of praise (albeit quietly because I am usually in a private corner of a public place). I jot down what God whispers to me in return. I clean out my mental pockets, set goals, and watch memorable movies of what God has done in my life over the past six months. And I also just sit, look at God's creation, and enjoy being in the presence of Someone I dearly love.

But setting aside one or two days a year to celebrate who God is and what He's done isn't big enough to hold what is excellent and praiseworthy. At least, it isn't for me—and it wasn't for the people of Israel.

From Sabbaths to Sundays

Two of the "big three" festivals God mandated for the people of Israel lasted a week or more. During these appointed times, God commanded His people to *"do no regular work"* (Numbers 28:18 and 26; 29:12). Add another divinely appointed day off for the Feast of Trumpets and Day of Atonement and you have a good chunk of a month every year set aside to help the people of Israel set their minds on what was excellent and praiseworthy. But there's more. There was also God's gift of the Sabbath.

Way back in the beginning, God ended His Genesis workweek with time for relaxation, contemplation, and celebration. After surveying His work and declaring it *"very good,"* Genesis 2:2–3 tells us that *"God blessed the seventh day and made it holy, because on it he rested from all the work of creating that he had done."* To make something *holy* means to set it apart, to make it distinctive. God set the seventh day aside as distinct and special from the rest of the week. In the Ten Commandments, God instructed His children to follow His example.

Once again, our slippery-fish Father, so often viewed as the harbinger of "thou shalt nots," shows Himself to be a God of "thou shalts." Our almighty God, who from what I've read never tires or sleeps, modeled for us how to refresh and refocus through holy celebration. And just like the children of Israel, we desperately need that refresher course. As mentioned before, our brains (and our bodies) need some downtime if they are to function at their best. Setting our work aside for awhile to focus on God's story, and our part in it, is a welcome way to do just that.

We are New Testament believers, not Old Testament Jews. But that doesn't mean we should cast off the lessons and laws found in the Old Testament as an outdated story that no longer applies to us. It is part of our history, part of His story given to teach, inspire, train, and point us in the direction of what is excellent and praiseworthy. Holy celebration is part of that story.

It's true we no longer celebrate the Jewish Sabbath. Instead, we commemorate Christ's resurrection each Sunday. But, how often does that fact come to mind? More likely, we regard Sunday simply as the day we go to church. We gather together as God's extended family for about an hour, sing a few songs, listen to the pastor expound on a portion of Scripture, perhaps partake of the Lord's Supper, and then head off our separate ways. We've done our duty. We've tipped our hat, our wallets, and perhaps our heart, to God. Now that we've fulfilled that obligation, it's time to make the most of our free time.

But what if we shifted our focus? What if, instead of viewing our Sunday service as an obligation, we viewed it as a time of celebration, a party held in God's honor? When we attend a birthday party or graduation ceremony for those we love, we don't ask, "What's in it for me?" We consider how we can best celebrate them. What would happen if we did the same for God?

Psalm 116:12–14 in *The Message* asks, *"What can I give back to GOD, for the blessings he's poured out on me? I'll lift high the cup of salvation—a toast to GOD! I'll pray in the name of GOD; I'll complete what I promised GOD I'd do, and I'll do it together with his people."* To me, this verse is the perfect picture of a praiseworthy Sunday. It progresses from me-focused to He-focused and then on to we-focused. It supports our ultimate goal: to love God and love others.

Choosing to focus on what is excellent and praiseworthy every Sunday (at least!) not only builds new associations in my brain between God and what is good, but with time it can forge new neural pathways. It can actually help me get in the habit of focusing more on God and less on me.

But I get an emotional kickback as a bonus. It's that whole Matthew 10:39 paradox: *"Whoever finds his life will lose it, and whoever loses his life for my sake will find it."* The more I focus on what is praiseworthy, the more grateful I feel. The more grateful I feel, the more buoyed my mood and the deeper my joy. The greater my joy, the more I want to return thanks—and the more inclined I am to want to return the favor. I want to offer the One who's blessed me so abundantly something precious in return. Each and every Sunday can be a touchstone that reminds me to do exactly that.

I consider my Sunday mornings a thank-you gift to God. Again, I happen to get a lot back in return. God often works that way. Pouring out my praise to God through song is downright fun. Catching a fresh glimpse of God's excellence and praiseworthiness through the pastor's message challenges me—and I enjoy a challenge. And (dare I admit it?) I even find myself getting a little excited over the offering.

Since my husband and I were first married, we decided we would give back to God at least 10 percent of our income, following the Old Testament touchstone of the tithe. It hasn't always been easy. One of our old weekly budget sheets from back in college lists these things under "assets": God, old groceries, Mark's wallet $40.00, Vicki's wallet $2.80. Our checks to the church weren't very big, but we watched God stretch our tiny budget in amazing ways. I won bagels and cream cheese on a radio show. Bags of groceries were left on our doorstep by friends. People at church would slip money into our back pockets when they gave us a hug. When we donated blood, we received coupons for free Big Macs, which we used for date nights.

It was a season of financial adventure. And that adventure continues. Holding loosely onto the resources God's given us while holding tightly onto God's faithfulness has helped open our eyes even wider to what is truly excellent and praiseworthy. Every Sunday, that offering bag is an invitation to place our security in God, instead of our finances. It's an invitation well worth accepting.

Whether it's through the offering, through song, through teaching Sunday School, through inviting a newcomer out to lunch, or through countless other opportunities to give to and through our local church, celebrating Sundays is just one more touchstone to add to our ever-growing collection. And we don't have to put that touchstone away when the benediction is done. Sunday isn't over yet.

Turning Holidays back into Holy Days

On the very first Sabbath day, God didn't take a quick breather to survey what He'd made and then jump right back into work. He set the entire seventh day apart from the rest of the week. I believe this example is both excellent and praiseworthy. It's a rather foreign concept worth letting our frazzled brains mull over for awhile.

In this modern day and age, we seem to not only be habitual multitaskers, but life-in-the-fast-lane celebrators. In the blink of an eye, we finish our Sunday morning worship service and hurry back home to catch up on email. We check off worship and celebration like another task on our to-do list. Our lives and our minds quickly refocus on things below. Why are we so hesitant to sit still for awhile—unless, of course, the TV happens to be blaring away in front of us?

Sunday is just one example. Consider Christmas and Easter. For our two traditional, God-centered celebrations, we shop, wrap, bake, eat, unwrap, clean up, and then mourn the time and money spent. In the midst of all the holiday hype and hubbub, we may wind up dedicating more time and attention to shopping for a new outfit to wear to Easter brunch or to our Christmas Eve service than we do to the actual service itself.

We briefly set our minds on what is excellent and praiseworthy about Christ's birth and resurrection, but we seem almost anxious to get things "back to normal." It's like we equate celebration with wasting time, because we don't get anything "important" accomplished.

When we reduce our holy days to holidays, we lose a precious touchstone. But most importantly, we begin to lose touch with God's big picture. We get so distracted with the details of throwing a party for ourselves that we forget to celebrate Him. We merely skim what is excellent and praiseworthy and head back to that small story, the one that revolves solely around us. In doing so, we trade things above for those below. We take another step toward forgetting the bigger picture we're a part of. And if we have children, there's even more at risk.

Ten days before the last, and most deadly, of the ten plagues swept across Egypt, God gave Moses and Aaron detailed instructions on how the Israelites should celebrate His provision of Passover for generations to come. Scripture details God's directives:

> *"When you enter the land that the* LORD *will give you as he promised, observe this ceremony. And when your children ask you, 'What does this ceremony mean to you?' then tell them, 'It is the Passover sacrifice to the* LORD, *who passed over the houses of the Israelites in Egypt and spared our homes when he struck down the Egyptians."*
> —Exodus 12:24–27

We celebrate not only for our sake, but for the sake of future generations. Consider my dear little two-year-old friend Lila. For Christmas, she received a toy ironing board as a gift from her grandparents. Squirming with excitement, Lila laid her gift flat on the ground, donned her bicycle helmet and kneepads, and then proceeded to surf her new "board" over the imaginary waves on the family room carpet.

In our permanent-press, dry-cleaner prolific world, Lila hasn't learned what an ironing board is for. Frankly, I feel that's no great loss. However, that same innocent ignorance could occur with future generations in regard to their understanding of who God is and what He's done if we do not model how to set our minds on what is excellent and praiseworthy. We have a duty to pass on what we've learned. To keep God's story alive. To slow down and wholeheartedly celebrate the big picture that is the foundation of our sacred celebrations.

My Personal Jubilee

We do not need a heavenly mandate to declare a time of celebration. Nehemiah threw a party when the rebuilding of the walls around Jerusalem was complete (Nehemiah 12:27). David *"danced before the LORD with all his might"* when the ark of the covenant arrived in Jerusalem (2 Samuel 6:14). Moses and his tambourine-tapping sister, Miriam, led the Israelites in song after walking through the Red Sea (Exodus 15:1–21). And in Jesus's parable of the prodigal son, the father prepares a magnificent feast to celebrate the return of his lost son (Luke 15:11–32).

These were more than impromptu potlucks and sing-alongs. These were deep-seated expressions of worship and praise. God and His praiseworthy excellence were at the center of each of these celebrations. We don't need to wait for something as life-changing as the return of a prodigal child to let our celebratory side shine through. Anything, big or small, that gives us cause for thanks can be cause for celebration.

A few years ago, I was reading in the Old Testament about the Sabbath year. The 25th chapter of Leviticus tells us that while God's people were instructed to celebrate the Sabbath every seventh day, every seventh year the people were to give the land a Sabbath rest. After seven Sabbath years (a total of 49 years), the 50th year was set aside as a Jubilee. This was a special time of trumpet blowing, freeing of slaves, forgiving of debts, and taking a break from working in the fields.

Considering I read Leviticus 25 right after my 49th birthday, this passage struck a personal chord with me. The big 5-0 was looming less than 12 months away, a milestone traditionally heralded by black balloons, gag gifts, and a general consensus that "it's all downhill from here." On the contrary, I felt as though my life was just getting started. So, I declared my own Sabbath year, followed by a personal Jubilee.

I didn't have any slaves to free or fields I could refuse to tend. I didn't have any financial debts to forgive, and figured our mortgage lender probably wouldn't consider forgiving the debt on our home. However, Leviticus inspired me to party. (Now, there's something you don't hear every day!) I celebrated what God had done in my life—and what He was going to do in and through me in the future.

For the next 24 months, I spent more time focusing on what was praiseworthy and less time trying to rustle up new freelance projects to fill my workdays to overflowing. I relaxed more, weighed myself less, and found myself actually looking forward to getting older. After all, here was a new frontier I hadn't yet explored. When my 730-day party came to a close, I found myself feeling a bit melancholy. I even asked God to allow me to live beyond the age of 99 so I could Jubilee all over again!

But we don't need a major time commitment, like two years, a week, or even a full day to declare a sacred celebration. I have an annual festival that lasts less than five minutes. Each year at the beginning of the Christmas season, I turn on a Trans-Siberian Orchestra CD and play the instrumental, "First Snow." While the electric guitars fill my family room with rollicking riffs, I lay on the couch with my eyes closed. In my mind, I'm dancing across the heavens, kicking up stars, and gliding over galaxies, all as an expression of thanks and praise to God. I'm not quite as uninhibited as David when it comes to dancing before the Lord, which is why I stick to the dance floor of my mind. (Even there, I resemble Snoopy from *Peanuts*, boogying atop his doghouse!) But, these few minutes fill my heart with incredible joy. Basking in the excellence of our praiseworthy God not only raises my spirits, but also helps center my Christmas season on what matters most.

Celebration can help us refocus on things above. It can act as a brake for our busy lives, slowing us down long enough to reflect on how God has come through for His children. It can help reveal the heights and depths of what is truly excellent and praiseworthy. It can change the way we think, the way we worship, and the way we greet each new day. It can help us join together with the psalmist in saying, *"I've thrown myself headlong into your arms—I'm celebrating your rescue. I'm singing at the top of my lungs, I'm so full of answered prayers"* (Psalm 13:5–6 *The Message*).

Deep "C" Fishing

Joy is not a continual state of bliss. It's more like a persistent call to praise. When we stop to take a closer look at who God is and what He's done, that call to us intensifies. Why not schedule your own day away with God to ponder the questions below—and venture out on the road to joy?

1. People are always talking about finding God's will. The Book of 1 Thessalonians is one place where we can find it. 1 Thessalonians 5:16–18 says, *"Be joyful always; pray continually; give thanks in all circumstances, for this is God's will for you in Christ Jesus."*

*   Why do you think being joyful, praying continually, and giving thanks are so important to God? Why, and how, are they important to you?

*   Do you think what 1 Thessalonians 5:16–18 tells us to do is realistic? How can setting our minds on what is excellent and praiseworthy help make this verse more of a reality in our lives?

*   A couple of friends of mine email a daily "gratitude list" back and forth to each other. One mentioned how writing and sharing what she's thankful for has helped open her

eyes a bit wider to what's truly praiseworthy in her life. Why do you think "counting your blessings" has a positive effect on your mood? What is one way you can become more aware of the blessings God brings into your life each day?

2. Celebrating Sundays, Christmas, Easter, or even our own personal Jubilee can be powerful touchstones for us, as well as precious gifts of worship for God. But they can also become something God despises.

"Stop bringing me your meaningless gifts; the incense of your offerings disgusts me! As for your celebrations of the new moon and the Sabbath and your special days for fasting—they are all sinful and false. I want no more of your pious meetings. I hate your new moon celebrations and your annual festivals. They are a burden to me. I cannot stand them!"
—Isaiah 1:13–14

- Why was God so upset over these celebrations? (Read the entire first chapter of Isaiah if you'd like to better understand the bigger story.)

- Why do you think how, and what, we celebrate is so important to God?

- How can we keep our celebrations pleasing and acceptable in God's eyes? Is there anything you'd like to change about how you celebrate Christmas, Easter, or Sunday?

- What effect would viewing our Sunday worship celebration as a gift to God have on any tendency we may have to complain about the music, sermon, or our church family? What possible effect might it have on our weekend "mood"?

3. Consider how you can use the touchstone of celebration to help you set your mind more solidly on what is excellent and praiseworthy.

- Make a list of your Top Ten blockbusters, times when you caught a glimpse of God at work in your life or in the world around you.

- Schedule a time to cry, eat, and "watch movies," featuring your list of blockbusters. Consider what is excellent and praiseworthy about God's role in each of these memories.

- Read Nehemiah 8 and 9, that describe the celebration Nehemiah and the people of Israel held after they rebuilt the walls of Jerusalem. What can you learn from their example? Why did Nehemiah tell the people, *"The joy of the LORD is your strength"* (Nehemiah 8:10)?

Part 3

TRANSFORMED
INTO
TOUCHSTONES

CHAPTER ELEVEN

ONLY THE BEGINNING

"Think about such things."
—Philippians 4:8

The story goes that Saint Augustine was walking along the beach one day pondering the weighty topic of the Trinity. But he wasn't alone. He saw a small boy running back and forth between the ocean waves and a hole in the sand, a bucket in his hand. When Augustine asked the boy what he was doing, the young lad said he was trying to put the ocean into the hole. Augustine chided the boy that it couldn't be done.

On further reflection, Augustine realized that he was trying to do the very same thing. He was trying to hold an infinite God within the confines of his finite brain. It was something that couldn't be done.

At this point, I think we'd all agree emphatically with Augustine. Through a single verse of Scripture, Philippians 4:8, we've filled our brains with a multitude of excellent and praiseworthy things above. But that's only the beginning. When Paul encourages us to think about *"such things"* it means his list is far from complete. We haven't even stuck our mental big toes into the infinite depths of such things as the Trinity, salvation, grace, heaven, or whether pretribulationism trumps posttribulationism. Frankly, at this point I already feel like the student in the *Far Side* cartoon who asks the teacher if he can please be excused because his brain is full.

I know I can attribute part of this struggle to my current season of life. The irony of a menopausal woman, who most days can't remember her own PIN number, writing a book on setting our minds firmly on anything, let alone on our slippery-fish God, is not lost on me. All I can say is it keeps me humble.

Each and every chapter of this book could be a book in itself. A really big book.

But our goal is not to exhaust the topics mentioned in Philippians 4 so we can cross them off our list. My hope is that this eclectic taste of things above whets our appetites for even more of what can't be seen, touched, or heard. And hopefully, along the way, we'll pick up a few helpful hints and habits that will better prepare our minds for what lies ahead.

Don't Just Change Your Mind—Change Your Brain

Over the course of the last ten chapters, we've gone fishing in waters we were never equipped to see the bottom of. With Philippians 4:8 as our fishing net, we've briefly caught hold of what is true, noble, right, pure, lovely, admirable, excellent, and praiseworthy. We've let these concepts squirm around under our mental microscopes for awhile. We've forged new cerebral connections by considering how these topics are relevant to us individually. We've strengthened our mental associations through elaboration and repetition as we've continued to integrate the use of touchstones into our daily lives. We've done exactly what Paul has asked us to do, *"think about such things."*

In Greek, the four words that conclude Philippians 4:8 are reduced to one: *logizomai*. This Greek word can mean "to use concentrated effort to put things together in our minds, to deliberately evaluate them over and over again." As we purposefully set our minds on things above, we're to calculate them, like a mathematical problem, putting them together with what we already know, seeing how they add up in light of Scripture.

There's a brainiac-sounding English term used in educational psychology that runs along the same lines as *logízomai*. It's *metacognition*. It's generally defined as "thinking about thinking" or "learning how to learn."

The premise behind metacognition is that when we pay attention to how we learn and remember things and then when we put what we know about those processes into practice, we can improve how well things stick in our brains. Sounds kind of self-intuitive to me.

However, the body of writing and research on this hot topic continues to grow. Some of it gets rather detailed and technical. But we don't need to fully understand metacognition to practice it. As a matter of fact, we've been using our metacognitive abilities throughout this book.

My own layperson's definition of *metacognition* is "to cogitate, calculate, and evaluate." We begin by doing what elementary school teachers remind their students to do each morning when that first bell rings. We put on our "thinking caps." We prepare ourselves to learn by becoming more conscious of what's going on in our heads through conscious cogitation. Then, we calculate how to best put what we know about how we learn into practice. We make a plan. For instance, we choose to use mnemonic devices such as repetition, elaboration, and relevance to help us remember. We even throw in a few personal touchstones for good mental measure.

The final step is for us to evaluate. Part of that takes place at the end of each chapter when we go "Deep 'C' Fishing." But as we near the end of this book, the time has come to ask ourselves what has worked for us and what has not. What touchstones have made a difference in how we think, act, and relate to God and others—and what touchstones have served as no more than souvenirs, cute little doodads we've picked up along our journey but that will wind up sitting on a mental shelf, gathering dust once the last page of this book is turned.

As for the forgettable doodads, toss 'em. Our brains and lives don't need any more clutter than we have to deal with already. What may be a valuable touchstone for me may be a mere mental trinket for you. Many of the personal touchstones I mention are shared for inspiration rather than imitation. Find what helps you set your mind on things above and then stick with it—until it doesn't work for you anymore. When that happens, toss it and find something else. Touchstones can become dated or so familiar that they are no longer useful.

That's why evaluation is important. As we regularly check in on our personal progress, we can make changes as needed, so we can keep moving forward. As for my own self-evaluation, I've already discarded a few touchstones I've written about in this book. Some of them served their purpose for a season. Others simply slipped my mind. No big surprise there. Sometimes, I need a reminder to remind me of what I'm using to help me remember!

Evaluation can serve as its own touchstone. It's like checking the map every so often when we're on an unfamiliar journey to make sure we're still headed in the proper direction. It gives us the opportunity to get back on track before we have a chance to wander too far off from our intended path. This is not only valuable when evaluating touchstones, but for evaluating the truth of anything new we learn about God and things above.

We can all take a lesson from the Bereans. Acts 17:10–12 says the believers from Berea were of *"noble character"* and received the gospel *"with great eagerness and examined the Scriptures every day to see if what Paul said was true."* I hope you're doing that as you read this book, evaluating it in light of Scripture. I do my very best to weigh what I write against what I know of God's Word. I may be wholeheartedly sincere, but I'm also wholly human. That means I'm fallible and my knowledge is limited. Both you and I have a responsibility to take 1 Thessalonians 5:21 seriously: *"Test everything. Hold on to the good."*

As we cogitate, calculate, and evaluate, we change more than our minds. We actually change the way we think. We forge new neural pathways in our brains. There was an ABC *20/20* television news special entitled "The Mystery of Happiness: Who Has It...How to Get It" that discussed how much control we have to change the way we think, particularly as it relates to being happy. In one study, participants spent a half hour each day thinking about compassion and kindness. Within only two weeks, there was a discernible change in their way of thinking. They began to demonstrate more kindness and compassion.

Imagine what a difference it would make if we spent just a half hour each day for the rest of our lives thinking about God and things above. Add the power of prayer and the work of God's Spirit and there's no way we could remain unchanged. We couldn't help but be *"transformed by the renewing"* of our minds (Romans 12:2). This process has nothing to do with the power of positive thinking. It's the power of a dynamic relationship with an almighty God. It's a miracle in the making, a Father too immense for our minds to contain, reaching down in love to change His children's lives from the inside out. In turn, as our lives and minds are transformed, we become touchstones for others.

LIFE IN THE SPOTLIGHT

Like every verse of Scripture, Philippians 4:8 does not stand alone. It has a context that cradles it, helping keep its truth intact from generation to generation. There is the whole of Scripture, the history and culture of the time when it was written, the personal experience of its author, Paul, and the rest of the letter to the Philippians in which this verse is found.

There are countless directions our minds could venture out and explore from this single starting point. But we're only going to look at one, the verse that follows Philippians 4:8. Frankly, this feels a bit like fishing in a stocked pond and being given only a one trout limit, but life is short—and so are our attention spans.

Paul writes in Philippians 4:9, *"Whatever you have learned or received or heard from me, or seen in me—put it into practice. And the God of peace will be with you."* At first reading, this can sound a bit presumptuous, as can similar statements Paul makes throughout his epistles, such as: *"I urge you to imitate me"* (1 Corinthians 4:16); *"I plead with you, brothers, become like me"* (Galatians 4:12); *"What you heard from me, keep as the pattern of sound teaching"* (2 Timothy 1:13); or *"Follow my example, as I follow the example of Christ"* (1 Corinthians 11:1).

The key to Paul's confidence in his own good example is found in the last phrase of 1 Corinthians 11:1, *"as I follow the example of Christ."* Christ is always the primary example we turn to. He is the first and foremost touchstone of our faith and His call to *"Follow Me"* rises above all others. But as we follow Him, we may find that others begin to follow us. They may lean on our lives and words as touchstones, using them as signposts to help guide them on their journey toward a closer relationship with God. Some may have officially begun this relationship, while others may still be checking out this God they've heard so much about. In other words, we're not only being watched, but sometimes imitated. That bears quite a responsibility—and can be a bit intimidating.

I had a neighbor who lived a few doors down from my family for almost a decade. One thing I felt fairly certain of was that here was a man who had little interest in things above. But several years after we moved away, my husband and I received a letter from our former neighbor. In it, he said he'd been watching our family closely for years and wanted us to know that what he saw helped him decide to follow Christ.

I can't remember ever having a deeply "spiritual" conversation with this man or doing anything saintlike in his presence. As a matter of fact, this season of our family's life was a time of intense struggle, not one I'd consider a shining beacon of perfection that I'd choose to put on display. But somehow, God used our family as a touchstone to point someone in the direction of eternity. For that, I am grateful, not to mention a bit amazed.

We don't have to be celebrities to live our lives in the public eye. Even if we never step onto a stage, hold a microphone in our hands, run for office, preach a sermon, or write a book, we may find ourselves being scrutinized. We risk admiration, or ridicule, just going about our daily lives. As we shop for groceries, make a new friend, join a church, get married, raise children, apply for a job, or drive our Yugo down the freeway, people make assumptions about who we are. And sometimes, those assumptions are far from accurate.

We cannot control what people think or say about us. Reputations can wax and wane according to how we're perceived and what others may choose to say behind our backs. We may suffer under the weight of criticism fired at us simply because others aren't privy to the big picture of our lives. They don't know us like God does—and that's OK. Proverbs 29:25 from *The Message* reminds us that *"the fear of human opinion disables; trusting in God protects you from that."*

We can't do much about our reputation. But we can do a lot about our character. With the help of God's Spirit, we can follow Christ's example, as well as the example of others whose lives and words are worthy of our admiration. We can take Paul's advice from Philippians 4:9 and put into practice what we learn. We can do our part in renewing our minds by intentionally pondering things above, using whatever touchstones help us along the way. We can celebrate the transformation God is working in our lives—and marvel at the fact that our individual transformation plays a part in transforming the entire body of God's church.

Living Stones, I Presume?

There is a cathedral in Barcelona that looks like an art nouveau fairy tale hewn in stone. But *La Sagrada Família*, "The Church of the Holy Family," preaches reality, not fantasy. Its eccentric architect, Antoni Gaudí, designed every element of his masterwork to "preach" a different portion of Scripture.

The Passion Facade tells the story of Christ's crucifixion and resurrection through expressionless faces chiseled onto angular figures. Around the corner, the Nativity Facade depicts Christ's childhood, where solid stone appears to drip like candle wax, forming almost indecipherable scenes (and inspiring me to nickname this the "Toxic Waste Facade.")

Inside the quirky cathedral, a forest of stone columns, reminiscent of the oaks of righteousness from Isaiah, reach skyward toward a ceiling of gargantuan stone leaves. Walls of stained glass praise the Light of the world, tingeing every cold, gray surface with warm kaleidoscope brilliance. An elevator to the roof reveals clumps of fruitlike mosaics clinging to spindly towers, as Galatians' "fruit of the Spirit" mimics Carmen Miranda's produce-filled headgear. Add the gargoyle-inspired lizards, snakes, frogs, dragons, and salamanders that crawl the exterior as Genesis-inspired waterspouts and your imagination can't help but begin writing its own surrealistic biblical tale—and questioning what your life would be like if God had given you a brain like Gaudí's.

But La Sagrada Família is far from complete. Intertwined with the fruit-topped towers and tree-trunk pillars, visitors find scaffolding, cranes, and other assorted construction materials and equipment. Since Gaudí's death in 1926 (after working on his masterpiece for 46 years), construction has continued, interpreted from Gaudí's models and drawings and paid for solely by private donation. It's estimated that another 30 to 80 years could pass before the final stone of La Sagrada Família is set in place.

Personally, I think the cathedral would preach a more powerful sermon if it remained as it has for over 100 years—

continually under construction. For on the Nativity Façade, a Latin dedication is carved into its exterior. Here Gaudí dedicated his magnum opus to the *"living stones"* who make up God's masterwork—His church.

First Peter 2:5 (NLT) says, *"And you are living stones that God is building into his spiritual temple."* Together we are building a uniquely quirky church for our heavenly Father; one pieced together with individuals more varied than the architectural elements that adorn La Sagrada Família, one that's under construction until the day that final trumpet sounds.

How far we allow God into our lives, how deeply we permit His hands to carve away the excess stone in our hearts and minds, helps determine the quality of the construction in our little corner of His church. *"If one part suffers, every part suffers with it; if one part is honored, every part rejoices with it,"* 1 Corinthians 12:26 explains to us in regard to how every individual part of God's church has an effect on the other.

What you do matters to me and what I do should matter to you. We are part of the same whole, the same body, the same church. We *"are no longer foreigners and aliens, but fellow citizens with God's people and members of God's household, built on the foundation of the apostles and prophets, with Christ Jesus himself as the chief cornerstone"* (Ephesians 2:20).

As living stones, we can fit together perfectly, like pieces in a jigsaw puzzle, or rub each other raw with our rough corners and irregular edges. What we allow ourselves to be conformed to will make all the difference. Will we conform to the world or be transformed into the image of Christ by the renewing of our mind? Will we become a touchstone or a stumbling block? Each decision we make is a swing of the chisel—and each decision begins with nothing more than a thought.

Deep "C" Fishing

So far, we've spent a lot of time cogitating and calculating. Now, it's time for a little evaluating. Look back over the chapters you've read so far. Reread anything you may have highlighted, as well as your answers to other "Deep 'C' Fishing" sections. Then consider the questions below:

1. Write a one-sentence touchstone for each chapter, summing up what you want to remember.

2. Philippians 4:8 has given us a lot to think about. Which of the seven topics we looked at from this verse had the deepest impact on you? Why?

3. How has what you've read changed the way you think? The way you act? The way you view God?

4. Is the concept of metacognition useful to you? If so, what's another area of your life you can apply it to?

5. If you've incorporated any touchstones into your life in the course of reading this book, which do you want to keep and which do you no longer need? Are there any touchstones you'd like to use, but haven't started yet? If so, what's holding you back?

CHAPTER TWELVE

LIFE AS A LIVING STONE

"The news of your faith in God is out. We don't even have to say anything anymore—you're the message!"
—1 Thessalonians 1:8 (*The Message*)

We've come full circle, back to the God who is a strong tower, a mighty warrior, a refuge, a shield, a solid rock—and a slippery fish. He remains too big for our minds to measure, His thoughts and ways too high for us to fully comprehend (Isaiah 55:9). But instead of shrugging our shoulders at our "big God, small brain" dilemma, we've joined the Colossians in accepting Paul's challenge to set our minds on things above. In doing so, we've begun an unparalleled journey—one that promises to transform our hearts, our words, our relationships, our actions, and even the inner workings of our brains.

The closer our journey takes us toward God, the more accurate a glimpse we get of our invisible Almighty. Yet, the more we come to know Him, the more we realize there is to know. Sometimes, it feels as though we're not making any headway. That's because comprehending the King and Creator of the universe is like trying to climb a mountain whose summit reaches to infinity.

I love the way author, pastor, and master paraphraser Eugene Peterson puts it in his book *A Long Obedience in the Same Direction*:

> "We would very soon become contemptuous of a god whom we could figure out like a puzzle or learn to use like a tool. No, if God is worth our attention at all, he must be a God we can look up to—a God we must look up to."
> —Eugene Peterson

But a funny thing happens as we continue gazing up at our God, pondering His immensity, struggling to grab hold of His slippery fish–like ways, pursuing whatever is true, noble, right, and beyond, and learning to walk in love with those we encounter along the way. We become more and more like the One we've set our minds on. We, too, become slippery fish.

From Awed to Odd

In the Bible, God is not the only one wrapped in metaphor. You and I are likened to living stones, salt, light, saints, priests, pilgrims, sheep, the bride of Christ, and a city on a hill. Second Corinthians 2:14 describes us as spreading *"the fragrance of the knowledge"* of Christ everywhere we go. We are the original Eternity cologne.

But I've found that the more increasingly "awed" I am with God, the more "odd" I become in the eyes of the world. I'm not only transformed into a potential touchstone, but a slippery fish, slithering out of the boundaries of what's perceived as normal. Consider our fishing net of Philippians 4:8. If I turn a deaf ear to gossip, choose to keep sex within the confines of marriage, freely give money to my church, and forgive those who've hurt me, I'm not going to fit the norm.

I'm in good company. The prophets and apostles as

described in Scripture certainly must have smelled a little "fishy" to their contemporaries. John the Baptist wore an ensemble made of camel hair, ate locusts and honey, and preached a radical life-change of confession, repentance, and baptism. Hosea followed God's direction to marry a prostitute, who Hosea continued to forgive and be reconciled to even after she committed adultery, as the prophet preached about Israel's unfaithfulness to God. Ezekiel lay on his left side for 390 days as a visual aid to illustrate to the people of Israel the 390 years they had turned away from God—then, promptly rolled over onto his right side for another God-ordained 40-day visual aid. Joshua marched his army and some trumpet-blowing priests around Jericho for seven days as God's battle plan for conquering the walled city of Jericho. And the prophet Isaiah, as directed by God, wandered around naked and barefoot for three years to show how the people of Egypt and Cush would be led away by the Assyrians.

As the prophet Isaiah said, *"Here am I, and the children the Lord has given me. We are signs and symbols in Israel from the Lord Almighty"* (Isaiah 8:18). In other words, "Here we are, God's children! We are touchstones, pointing the way toward our almighty God and 'things above.'" Considering how outlandish the words and actions of God's followers may have seemed, how could people help but look... and consider.

Fast-forward to today. Now, God's Spirit indwells all who believe, not just working in a few chosen prophets. As His children, we remain *"signs and symbols,"* but in a less literal way than was needed before the coming of Christ and completion of Scripture. God may still call us to do things we may consider uncomfortable and that others may consider unconventional, but I believe the days of eating locusts and wandering around naked in the name of the Lord are over. Serving, loving, forgiving—these are the kind of visual aids God is most likely to call us to today.

If we are signs and symbols that point the way to God, we should be people whose lives are worth admiring. People whom others can look up to and learn from. Not for our glory, but for God's. We should be people who can join together with the prophet Isaiah in saying, *"Your name and renown are the desire of our hearts"* (Isaiah 26:8).

Remember, what is lovely or noble invites and attracts, drawing others toward love and right relationship. But it's also true that the fragrance of Christ we spoke of from 2 Corinthians 2:14 can be perceived as an *"aroma of death"* (2 Corinthians 2:15–16 NKJV) by those who have no interest in knowing God. It can actually repel some people we come into contact with, without us doing anything repellent. We've learned from Scripture that Christ will be a stumbling block for some people. But that's not what we should be. As living stones, we should be touchstones pointing toward things above, not millstones that hinder another's journey toward God.

While it's true that we may appear a bit odd if we don't conform to the world around us, we shouldn't automatically label ourselves as "under persecution" if someone rolls his or her eyes at us and turns away. It may a sign that we need a little God-inspired checkup. Perhaps a self-righteous or judgmental attitude is creeping in and motivating us to throw stones, instead of becoming beautiful living stones.

People we interact with each and every day continue to search for the meaning of life, for the gift of true love, and for the existence of a higher power. Others may have a relationship with God, but are deeply in need of another living stone to help them grow or heal or simply help carry their load for awhile. As living touchstones to things above, we can ask God for wisdom in how we can best point others back up to Him. At times, His answer may be found in handing them a touchstone of their own.

The Heart Rock Café and Oasis
Sometimes we choose a touchstone. Sometimes God drops one in our very own backyard. Literally. At least that's what

happened to me. When my husband and I moved to Phoenix, we were entering our empty-nest stage. That meant it was time to downsize. Well, at least that was the plan.

But Mark and I have this odd habit of inviting people into our home—friends, family, total strangers. Sometimes they spend the night. Sometimes they stay for months. So when we chose a home in Phoenix, we chose one with guests in mind. On the day we moved in, I went from room to room, asking God to transform our new home into a place where people's hearts could heal. It wasn't something I'd planned on doing. It simply felt like it was something God wanted me to do.

I first glimpsed an answer to my prayer the day workers pieced together a "water feature" for our backyard. When the day's work was done, I went out to inspect our new waterfall, constructed from a wheelbarrow full of random boulders. I immediately did a double take. The right side of the waterfall was made up of a single stone in the shape of a heart—with a crack running right down the center. Better yet, this "heart in need of healing" was positioned directly across from our guest room window.

In honor of God's massive touchstone, Mark and I dubbed our guest room the Heart Rock Café and Oasis. Since its grand opening, our oasis has welcomed guests from all walks of life. Harried moms in need of a quiet retreat. Strangers in town for a conference or counseling. A friend of a friend running a local marathon.

And so very many hearts in need of healing. Each visit is unique. Each life story different. Each guest, a gift I have the privilege of praying for.

Along with a comfy bed, a basket filled with Arizona maps and travel information, and a "dress for the next guest" Mr. Potato Head, we've placed two bowls of river rocks in our guest oasis. One bowl holds rocks engraved with words like *joy, pray, inspire,* and, of course, *heal.* At one time, there was even one that read, *You rock!* The other bowl is filled with unmarked stones, waiting to be written upon.

We invite our guests to choose an engraved stone to take home with them, a reminder of something God had shown them during their time in Phoenix. In turn, we asked them to leave a word of thanks to God or a message for future guests written in marker on one of the stones in the opposite bowl.

It's such a small thing, but God has used those stones, and our home, in amazing ways. Each and every story is worth telling, but they are not my stories to tell. However, one thing I can share is that one of our guests had the image of a phoenix tattooed on his ankle because his visit to Phoenix was such a spiritually significant time for him to rise from the ashes of the past. Sometimes, a little engraved rock just isn't a big enough touchstone.

The concept of our Heart Rock Café and Oasis grew along with the desire my husband and I had for our guests to do more than just "vacation" in our home. Our prayer was that our guests would see God more clearly during their stay in Phoenix, regardless of whether they believed in Him or not. Once we have explained the bowl of touchstones to our guests, we've found many of them set several aside at the beginning of their visit. Right before they leave, they evaluate the time they've had and choose which word best describes what they want to remember to set their minds on more regularly. Sounds like metacognition to me!

When we come across something that inspires us, amazes us, or makes a positive difference in our lives, we want to share it. We do it all the time with little things like recipes, diet tips, or the name of a new book we've enjoyed. So, why not pass on our favorite touchstones?

I've found that touchstones can make meaningful (and often inexpensive!) gifts. When I was moving to Phoenix, I wanted to give my circle of friends in Colorado a gift to express how much they meant to me, as well as remind them how much they meant to God. But money was tight.

While packing, I found lots of keys that went to who knows what. I tried doors, suitcases, bicycle locks—all to no avail. Instead of throwing them away, I turned the keys into touchstones. With a bright piece of ribbon, I tied a key to a 3-by-5 card with Matthew 16:19 written on it: *"Jesus said, 'I will give you the keys to the kingdom of heaven.'"* I told my friends that I didn't want them to forget the importance of the key Jesus offered them as easily as I had forgotten what these keys were meant to open. And when it came to the kingdom of heaven, I'd see them there, if not before.

Passing on a verse of Scripture, a word of encouragement, or a memento that points others toward things above may seem like a small thing, but it's a small thing wrapped in the hands of a very big, and very creative, God. We never know what God will use to change the course of someone's life. The more our own minds and lives are transformed, the more we'll find we have to share with others—and the more we'll find ourselves drawn to share.

Every Living Stone Has a Story

Kerosene or cold water—one or the other often seems to be thrown onto the fire of casual conversation when the subject of politics or religion enters a discussion. With such emotionally charged topics, it's easy to slip from dialogue into monologue. After all, our side deserves to be heard. But as we climb onto our soapbox or into our pulpit, our conversation begins to sound more like a campaign or crusade. Everyone involved feels the pressure to choose sides, even if they haven't really decided which side they are on. And once we choose a side, we feel obligated to defend it. We need to prove we made the right decision. We need to win.

Some people enjoy this kind of verbal boxing match. Not me. That's why I rarely discuss politics or religion. As for God, well, He's another matter altogether. I can talk about Him all day long. If I can't keep quiet about a great new restaurant I've found or movie I've seen, how can I possibly remain silent about how God is radically transforming my life?

I guess I feel a bit like John. The disciple often referred to as *"the disciple Jesus loved"* writes these words about what he witnessed:

> *"That which was from the beginning, which we have heard, which we have seen with our eyes, which we have looked at and our hands have touched—this we proclaim concerning the Word of life.... We proclaim to you what we have seen and heard, so that you may have fellowship with us. And our fellowship is with the Father and with his son, Jesus Christ. We write this to make our joy complete."*
> —John 1:1, 3–4

John couldn't help but share the amazing things he'd seen, heard, and even touched. I haven't had the opportunity to see, hear, or touch Jesus firsthand, but that doesn't mean I haven't had an encounter with God. Like John, I want to share that life-changing experience with others, drawing them closer in relationship to both God and myself. Sharing that story helps complete my joy.

We all have a story to tell, one with God at its center. Some may read like adventures, while others may resemble mysteries or tender love stories. These stories are much bigger than how we first "became a Christian." They include the personal blockbusters God has written into our lives, as well as the struggles we're still battling. They hold unanswered questions and wrong choices, as well as victories and revelations. They recount times of rending our garments in sorrow, as well as all-out joyous celebration. Ours are stories without any ending, stories whose intricate plots will continue long after our bodies have been laid to rest.

We often refer to these stories as testimonies because they are reminiscent of a witness testifying in court as to what he or she has seen, heard, and touched. In Acts 1:8, Jesus's final words to those who choose to follow Him exhort us to be witnesses throughout the world. Our own stories are a continuation of the Book of Acts. As these stories are ongoing, so should be our witness. Every day there's more for us to tell. The more we set our minds on things above, the more evidence we'll uncover about who God is and how He moves.

Some people are rather timid about sharing their God story with others. Some feel their story isn't sensational enough to be significant or that they aren't knowledgeable enough to adequately answer questions others may have about God. Jesus called us to be His witnesses, not His defense attorneys. We don't have to prove beyond a reasonable doubt His existence, sovereignty, or all-encompassing goodness to anyone. We simply have to testify to what we've experienced; what we've seen, heard, felt, and tasted of God and His Word in this world.

The best witness is someone who has paid attention to the matter at hand, taken mental note of the details, mulled them over to make sure they are correct in his or her mind, and then relates the whole story of his or her encounter in a clear, concise way that others can easily understand. That's all we have to do; tell what we know. That may involve answering some questions, like any witness is asked to do on the witness stand. But, that doesn't mean we have to know it all—because we don't. And we can't. If we pretend like we have God and things above all figured out, and those listening to our story decide to follow God, imagine how confused they'll be when they are confronted with the fact that He's a slippery fish!

God has given some of His witnesses the spiritual gift of evangelism. These people may be a whiz at apologetics, able to debate theology in a way that doesn't intimidate but instead illuminates, attracting and inviting others toward a deeper understanding of God. This is not a gift He's given me. That doesn't give me a hall pass for life, excusing me from telling others what I've experienced in relation to God. In the first chapter of Acts, Jesus called all of His followers, which includes you and me, to be witnesses. That means we need to rise up and open our mouths. After all, the book is called, "Acts," not "Sits Like a Bump on a Log."

God is daily put on trial by many people who are seeking truth in this world. Our testimony can be an accessible touchstone for them, providing evidence of things above. Isaiah 43:12 tells us, *"'You are my witnesses,' declares the LORD, 'that I am God.'"* Our responsibility isn't to convince others of God's truth. That's where the Holy Spirit comes in. All we need to do is be reliable witnesses.

I love how my husband responded to two very scientific-minded seatmates during a recent flight on a business trip. Their conversation had turned to things above, and the men questioned how an intelligent man like my husband could believe in a God who was, well, such a slippery fish. Mark replied, "I don't understand everything about God and the Bible, but I've found there's enough that I do understand and believe that I'm able to have faith for the rest."

My husband's conversation didn't spark a midflight conversion experience, but it did encourage an open and authentic discussion about the meaning of faith. That happens a lot with my husband when he flies. I don't think God has given Mark the spiritual gift of evangelism, but I do see Mark as a faithful witness to what God's done in his life. And after a conversation with Mark, I find most people are hungry to hear more. That's God's "salt of the earth" quality coming out in him.

How We Leave

Out of all the metaphors Jesus used to describe His followers, I think my favorite is the salt of the earth. Anytime I hear this phrase, my quirky little mind paints a picture of me as a tortilla chip for things above. Personally, I find tortilla chips addictive. Contrary to popular advertising, when it comes to potato chips, I *can* eat just one. But tortilla chips? No chance.

I want tortilla chip qualities in my life. I want to invite and attract others in a way that will verge on addictive. Not because I'm such a clever or attractive hunk of deep-fried tortilla, but because my words and actions hold just the right amount of salt. I long for others who spend time with me to find themselves growing more and more thirsty for the Living Water only Jesus can provide.

I believe that the more I consistently set my mind on things above, the closer my saltiness will get to being in that Goldilocks range of "just right." But every bag of chips, tortilla or otherwise, has an expiration date. And so do I. I believe even that realization can be a touchstone. For it's not only how we live, but how we leave this earth that points the way toward things above.

A while back, I had a funky fainting spell, accompanied by some weird sensory perception problems. My doctor scheduled an MRI. She told me not to worry, but that a brain tumor was one possible diagnosis for my symptoms. What amazed me was that I could actually do what my doctor suggested. I didn't worry. God felt so close and I felt so at peace, regardless of what the final outcome would be.

As I waited by the phone for the results of the MRI, a lot of thoughts were going through my mind. I considered what life would be like for my husband and my kids if my condition were terminal. I thought of weddings I'd never attend and grandchildren I might not have the opportunity to hold. I thought of books I'd never have the chance to write. I thought how much I really love life.

Then I began thinking of heaven. I thought of meeting Jesus, of worshipping Him in total abandon without worrying what others might think, of finally seeing, hearing, and touching the One who's in a realm beyond my mortal senses. I thought what it would be like to grasp the slippery fish of my Lord with both hands and shout, "I get it! I finally get it!"

When the phone rang and I learned that the MRI showed a perfectly healthy brain, I was surprised by my immediate reaction. I felt elation and relief in knowing my time on earth wasn't yet at an end. But right before that flashed a lightning-quick burst of tears and a sharp pang of sorrow. I had so wanted to finally know God in a way I knew was impossible while I'm still here on earth.

That brief moment has helped shape the way I feel about the future. I'm right there with Paul in Philippians 1:21 when he says, *"For to me, to live is Christ and to die is gain."* Once again, in the world's view this is downright odd. But to me, it's a cry of freedom.

That's one reason why planning my funeral doesn't seem like a morbid thing for a healthy woman in her 50s to do. That's where seashells come in. If you'll think back to the third chapter, you'll recall that a seashell was the very first touchstone God brought my way right after I committed my life to following Him. Throughout the years, particularly during tough times, seashells have turned up for me in unexpected places. They have become treasured touchstones, reminders of God's presence and care throughout part 1 of the story of my life.

It's only fitting they should herald my journey into part 2, for what is a seashell but a discarded home? It's a residence that's no longer needed, a touchstone to a story that's already been told. On that day when I finally meet Jesus face-to-face, I'll cast off my body like a fragile shell. And my hope is that those who happen to join in celebrating my passing from this life to the next will leave with a shell of their own, a touchstone for them to things above, a reminder that a heavenly Heart Rock Café and Oasis awaits us all, a home where we will be healed and whole.

However, even in heaven, I think God will remain a bit of a slippery fish. I know that 1 Corinthians 13:12 tells me, *"Now we see but a poor reflection as in a mirror; then we shall see face to face. Now I know in part; then I shall know fully, even as I am fully known."* I may finally know God fully, but that doesn't necessarily mean I'll comprehend Him completely. For God will be still be God—and I will not.

The beauty is that I will no longer forget. God and things above will be right there, continually within my reach. I will finally see the One that, so far, I've viewed only through my mind's eye. Whatever is true, noble, right, pure, lovely, admirable, and praiseworthy will no longer be concepts I struggle to hold in my mind and heart. They'll be my new address. As for touchstones, they'll be a thing of the past, reminders I no longer need. I'll cast them, along with crowns, before God's feet—and discover what it truly means to rejoice.

Deep "C" Fishing

Congratulations! You've given your mind, and hopefully your faith, quite a workout. As Colossians 2:6–7 in *The Message* says, *"You know your way around the faith. Now do what you've been taught. School's out; quit studying the subject and start living it! And let your living spill over into thanksgiving."*

1. Begin your time with God in thanksgiving. Thank Him for how He's revealed Himself to you, for what you know, as well as what you don't.

• Do you consider God more, or less, of a slippery fish after reading this book? What areas do you feel are the "slipperiest"?

Colossians 2:2–4 (*The Message*) says, *"I want you woven into a tapestry of love, in touch with everything there is to know of God. Then you will have minds confident and at rest, focused on Christ, God's great mystery. All the richest treasures of wisdom and knowledge are embedded in that mystery and nowhere else. And we've been shown the mystery! I'm telling you this because I don't want anyone leading you off on some wild-goose chase, after other so-called mysteries, or 'the Secret.'"*

• Obviously, what we set our minds on matters. We may not understand it all, but what we do understand of our slippery-fish God promises to provide our minds with confidence and rest—and guard our hearts from chasing wild geese. How do you think this works?

2. God has set you apart, like the prophets and the apostles, to be a *"living stone,"* an irreplaceable part of His church, a touchstone that points others toward things above.

• Can you think of a time when you were a touchstone to things above for someone else?

• Who has been a living stone you have watched closely, and perhaps tried to imitate, in your life?

• Is there any way you might be considered "odd" in the eyes of the world? Is this a positive thing?

• If you were asked to share your testimony, what would you say? How can you incorporate some of your personal blockbusters into your God story?

3. First Peter 1:4 in *The Message* says, *"We've been given a brand-new life and have everything to live for, including a future in heaven—and the future starts now!"*

- How does having a future in heaven make a difference in your life today?

BIBLIOGRAPHY

Chapter 2
Matthew, Kathryn. "Romance Rehab." *O Magazine*, May 2007. Quoting Norman Doidge, MD (author of *The Brain That Changes Itself*).

Gibb, Barry J. *The Rough Guide to the Brain*. London: Rough Guides Ltd., 2007.

Garcia, Leslie. "5 Ways to Strengthen Your Brain." *Dallas Morning News*, May 21, 2007.

www.mamashealth.com/

www.at-bristol.org.uk/

www.brainconnection.com

www.idahoptv.org/

www.jwhitchurch.home.insightbb.com/

www.thethinkingbusiness.co.uk/

Chapter 4
Matthew Henry's Commentary on the Old Testament. Electronic STEP Files, 2005. Quick Verse, Genesis 15:17.

Douglas, J. D. *New Commentary on the Whole Bible: New Testament*. Electronic STEP Files, 2005. Quick Verse, Matthew 16:17.

Chapter 5
Ritter, Malcolm. "Science Finally Pays Attention to Not Paying Attention." *Arizona Republic*, March 20, 2007.

www.cybercollege.com/

Zodhiates, Spiros, ed. *The Complete Word Study Dictionary: New Testament*. Chattanooga: AMG, 1992.

www.oprah.com/

www.invisiblechildren.com/

Chapter 6
Zodhiates, Spiros, ed. *The Complete Word Study Dictionary: New Testament*. Chattanooga: AMG, 1992.

Chapter 7
Zodhiates, Spiros, ed. *The Complete Word Study Dictionary: New Testament*. Chattanooga: AMG, 1992.

The 100 Most Important Bible Verses. Nashville: The W Publishing Group, 2005.

www.straightdope.com/

Chapter 8
Zodhiates, Spiros, ed. *The Complete Word Study Dictionary: New Testament.* Chattanooga: AMG, 1992.

Chapter 9
Nature magazine, February 1, 2005. www.primates.com/

Chapter 11
Zodhiates, Spiros, ed. *The Complete Word Study Dictionary: New Testament.* Chattanooga: AMG, 1992.

www.gse.buffalo.edu/

www.members.iinet.net.au/

http://coe.sdsu.edu/

www.en.wikipedia.org/

http://tip.psychology.org/

ABC News *20/20*, "The Mystery of Happiness: Who Has It and How to Get It," January 11, 2008.

Chapter 12
Peterson, Eugene. *A Long Obedience in the Same Direction.* 2nd ed. Downers Grove, IL: InterVarsity Press, 2000, 63.

Go Even Deeper with These Books
from New Hope

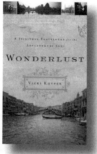

Wonderlust
A Spiritual Travelogue for the
Adventurous Soul
Vicki J. Kuyper
ISBN: 1-59669-076-3

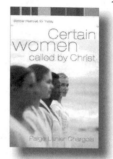

Certain Women
Called by Christ
Biblical Realities for Today
Paige Lanier Chargois
ISBN: 1-59669-200-6

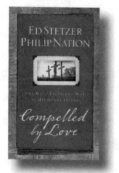

Compelled by Love
The Most Excellent Way
to Missional Living
Ed Stetzer and Philip Nation
ISBN: 1-59669-227-8

Splash the Living Water
Sharing Jesus in
Everyday Moments
Esther Burroughs
ISBN: 1-59669-002-X

Available in bookstores everywhere

For information about these books or any New Hope product,
visit www.newhopepublishers.com.